JOSEPH CAROLA, SJ

Conformed to Christ Crucified

Volume Two

More Meditations on Priestly Life and Ministry

D1557222

GREGORIAN & BIBLICAL PRESS

Cover: Serena Aureli
Layout: Scuola Tipografica S. Pio X - Roma   .

Cover sheet image: © Giovanni Battista Gaulli (detto "il Baciccia"), *Morte di San Francesco Saverio* (sec. XVII), Chiesa di S. Andrea al Quirinale in Roma

Back cover photo: Mark Jensen/University of St. Thomas

© 2015 Pontifical Biblical Institute
Gregorian & Biblical Press
Piazza della Pilotta 35, 00187 - Roma
www.gbpress.net - books@biblicum.com

ISBN 978-88-7839-**310**-3

A. M. D. G.

*For my mother and father
my first teachers and indeed my best teachers
in the ways of faith.*

Requiescant in pace.

For Zach Sandquist,
may the good Lord
bless you,
Father Joseph Carola, S.J.
Rome, 15 . IX . 2015

CONTENTS

Acknowledgments   9

Introduction   11

PART ONE

HOLY ORDERS

I.   The Waters at Meriba   19
        Choosing life in Christ

II.   Armed with a Two-edged Sword   23
        Believing, teaching and living the revealed Word of God

III.   The Call of Saint Matthew   29
        Preaching the Gospel of Mercy according to Caravaggio

IV.   Saint Bruno and Evangelical Simplicity   35
        Abandoning all things to follow Christ

V.   Christ Jesus the Celibate High Priest   49
        *Loving our neighbour as Christ Jesus has loved us from
        the Cross*

VI.   Saint Martha and Saint Mary   59
Magnanimously serving the Lord

VII.   A Blessed Breaking on Verdant Pastures   77
Serving the Lord faithfully in our poverty

VIII.   The Priesthood and the Cross   89
Bearing the other's burden in imitation of Christ Crucified

IX.   A First Mass of Thanksgiving, Brainerd   95
Ministering Word and Sacrament both in and out of season

X.   A Mass of Thanksgiving, Rome   101
Faithfully celebrating the sacred mysteries

PART TWO

RELIGIOUS LIFE

XI.   Amor Meus   109
Faithfully following the Incarnate Word

XII.   The Mystery of the Lamb   119
Wounded, I will never cease to love

XIII.   The Holy House and the Holy Habit   123
Putting on Christ in the service of the Gospel

PART THREE

THE PASCHAL MYSTERY

XIV.   Saint Clement of Rome, Lent 2010   131
       Presiding in love

XV.   Saint Clement of Rome, Lent 2011   137
       Living Christian unity

XVI.   Saint Clement of Rome, Lent 2013   141
       Chastening the body to heal the soul

XVII. Saint Clement of Rome, Lent 2014   145
       Yearning for God like the deer for running streams

XVIII. Saint Clement of Rome, Lent 2015   149
       Remaining in the Truth of Christ

XIX.   Christ Tempted in the Desert   155
       Humbly persevering in the priesthood

XX.   Lenten Vespers   165
       Running so as to win the incorruptible crown of eternal life

XXI.   Saint Thomas the Apostle   171
       Joyfully professing the paschal faith within the Church

ACKNOWLEDGMENTS

I wish to thank Jeffrey Cole of the Midwest Theological Forum for having suggested this second volume of *Conformed to Christ Crucified* at the time of the first volume's publication. His words of encouragement planted the seed for this second collection of meditations. I am grateful to Katia Paoletti of the Gregorian & Biblical Press and the Reverend James Socias for making this present publication possible. I want to thank the Reverend Gabriele White of the Family of Mary, the Reverend Justin Kizewski and Mr. Garrett Ahlers for carefully proof-reading the manuscript. My thanks go to the seminarians, deacons and priests of the Pontifical North American College who invited me to direct their retreats, preach at their Holy Hours and celebrate the annual Lenten stational Mass at the Church of San Clemente. I offer my thanks as well to the students and staff at San Luigi dei Francesi and the Almo Collegio Capranica for their respective invitations to preach to their communities during Lent. I am particularly grateful to the Reverend Thom Hennen and the Reverend Michael DeAscanis for the invitation to preach at the seminarian convocations of their respective dioceses during the summer of 2014. I also want to thank the Reverend Carlo Devoto, the Reverend Seth Gogolin and the Reverend Michael Pawlowicz who requested that I preach during the celebrations surrounding their sacerdotal ordinations. A word of thanks rightly goes as well to Mother Mary Clare, ACJ, the Foundress of the Handmaids of the

Heart of Jesus, for inviting me to celebrate the Mass of Investiture for two novices of the community. I am deeply grateful for the friendship of the Religious Sisters of the Incarnate Word and Blessed Sacrament in Houston, Texas, and the Little Sisters of the Lamb in whose communities I have always received a warm welcome. I am also thankful for the friendship and support of Mauro Cardinal Piacenza and Raymond Cardinal Burke. Finally, I extend my heartfelt thanks to Pope Emeritus Benedict XVI for the support which he has offered privately for this second volume of *Conformed to Christ Crucified*. His theological vision, papal magisterium and indeed friendship have greatly inspired what these pages contain.

INTRODUCTION

Conformed to Christ Crucified: Meditations on Priestly Life and Ministry appeared in 2010 during the *Year for Priests* inaugurated by Pope Benedict XVI. Since its publication, I have continued to preach to seminarians and priests as well as to Religious and the lay faithful on similar themes pertaining to priestly life and ministry. This second volume of *Conformed to Christ Crucified* gathers together these more recent homilectic meditations (with the sole exception of Sermon I which dates from 2003). The Scriptures read within the Church's living Tradition remain their primary inspiration. My own priestly life and ministry over the past five years, however, have also profoundly shaped these sermons. After the death of a Jesuit confrere and colleague in November of 2010, my duties at the Gregorian University increased dramatically. I managed to sustain that intense workload for almost two years, but by the Spring of 2012 my own health began to fail. During the years which followed, I learned much about what it means to serve the Lord in humility. In doing so I have also discovered the true meaning of magnanimity in priestly ministry.

Holy Orders sacramentally conform priests to Christ Crucified. Bearing our cross in the service of others, we do indeed suffer. If we attempt to bear that cross without the aid of Christ's grace, it cripples us. But if we seek His grace prudently and prayerfully, we experience His Cross for what It truly is: the Tree of Life. Elaborating upon this spiritual

11

insight, the sermons in this collection repeatedly return to the Philippians hymn of Christ's self-abasement. That hymn lauds His death upon the Cross, but it does not conclude there. Rather, it joyfully proclaims that "God has highly exalted him and bestowed on him the name which is above every name, that at the name of Jesus every knee should bow, in heaven and on earth and under the earth, and every tongue confess that Jesus Christ is Lord, to the glory of God the Father" (Philippians 2:9-11).[1] To be conformed to Christ Crucified, therefore, is to be conformed to the Living One who is not to be found among the dead (cf. Luke 24:5). It is to be conformed to the *Risen* Lord Jesus Crucified who is Wounded Love Victorious.

The present collection is divided into three parts: (1) *Holy Orders*, (2) *Religious Life* and (3) *The Paschal Mystery*. Part One contains sermons preached with explicit reference to the life and ministry of priests. Part Two treats themes of Christian discipleship and the Religious life. While the sermons in this second section were preached to communities of women Religious, they are also applicable to priests whether they be diocesan or Religious themselves. Part Three, as the title suggests, includes meditations preached during Lent and Easter.

Found in Part One, Sermons I – III were preached to North American seminarians at Holy Mass during their annual retreat. Sermons IV – V were preached in the domestic

---

[1] All biblical quotations are taken from the Revised Standard Version, Catholic edition, unless otherwise indicated.

chapel of the Pontifical North American College located within the Vatican City's extraterritorial zone during Eucharistic Holy Hours dedicated to the spiritual formation of candidates for the transitional diaconate. Sermons VI – VII are conferences which were given at seminarian convocations for the Archdiocese of Baltimore, America's premier see, and the four dioceses of the State of Iowa. They are the direct spiritual fruit of the health challenges mentioned above. Sermons VIII – X were preached on the occasion of the sacerdotal ordinations of Father Carlo Devoto of the Archdiocese of Cagliari in Sardinia, Father Seth Gogolin of the Diocese of Duluth in Minnesota and Father Michael Pawlowicz of the Diocese of Joliet in Illinois. The first of these sermons was preached originally in Italian in the parish church of Saints Peter and Paul in Cagliari on the vigil of Father Devoto's ordination. The second was preached in the parish church of Saint Andrew in Brainerd during Father Gogolin's First Mass of Thanksgiving. The third was preached at a Mass of Thanksgiving which Father Pawlowicz offered at the Basilica of San Pancrazio for his friends in Rome.

As we noted above, Part Two consists of sermons preached to Religious Sisters. Sermon XI was preached for the Religious Sisters of the Incarnate Word and Blessed Sacrament of Houston, Texas, in their Motherhouse chapel as the Sisters were about to begin their annual retreat. The Sisters had taught me and my siblings in our youth. In many ways I myself am a Religious today because of the faithful witness of Sister Rosalia Purcell, C.V.I. Sermon XII was preached at the Santi Quattro Coronati convent of the Little

Sisters of the Lamb in Rome. Catholic Studies students from the University of Saint Thomas in Saint Paul, Minnesota, had gathered there that evening for Holy Mass in order to celebrate the birthday of one of their members who had been recently injured in an accident. Sermon XIII was preached for the investiture of two novices of the Handmaids of the Heart of Jesus of the Diocese of New Ulm in Minnesota. The Mass of Investiture took place in the crypt chapel of the Shrine of the Holy House of Loreto in the Abruzzi region of Italy.

Found in Part Three, *The Paschal Mystery*, Sermons XIV – XVIII, are a collection of homilies preached over various years on the second Monday of Lent in the Station Church of Saint Clement of Rome. Given that the Scripture readings remain always the same for that day of Lent, I have had to exercise a certain creativity when choosing appropriate themes. Sermons XIV and XV consider the saints of the basilica: Saint Clement of Rome, Saint Ignatius of Antioch, and Saints Cyril and Methodius. Sermon XVI meditates upon the propers of the Mass for that day of Lent. Sermon XVII explains one particular scene in the apse mosaic, and Sermon XVIII considers the complementary nature of justice and mercy. Nonetheless, the Scriptures of the day remain the meditations' constant inspiration.

Sermon XIX was preached on the First Sunday of Lent for the priests of San Luigi dei Francesi (the residence of French priests studying in Rome) who had gathered in retreat at the Venerable English College's villa at Palazzola just across from Castel Gandolfo on Lago Albano. Preached originally in French for French-speaking priests by an American Jesuit at an English villa in the Italian countryside, this sermon clearly attests to the universality of the Catholic Church which we live daily at the heart of the Church in Rome. Sermon XX was preached originally in Italian during Second Vespers for the Third Sunday of Lent at the Almo Collegio Capranica, one of the three seminaries belonging to the Diocese of Rome and, in fact, the oldest seminary in the Church, predating the reforms of the Council of Trent. Finally, Sermon XXI was composed at the request of Mauro Cardinal Piacenza, the then-Prefect of the Congregation for the Clergy, to be posted on the Congregation's webpage during the *Year of Faith* 2012-2013.

FATHER JOSEPH CAROLA, S.J.
The Pontifical Gregorian University, Rome
19 March 2015
The Solemnity of Saint Joseph,
Spouse of the Blessed Virgin Mary

PART ONE

HOLY ORDERS

I

THE WATERS AT MERIBA
Choosing life in Christ

Reading: Baruch 1:15-22
Gospel: Luke 10:13-16

At Meriba on the day of Massah, God commanded
Moses to bring forth water from the rock to quench the Israelites' thirst. Satisfied only momentarily, they soon forsook
God's ways. Their hearts went astray. Therefore, in His anger,
God swore: "They [shall] not enter into my rest" (Psalm
95:11). If there are words no more beautiful to the human
ear than those words which the Crucified Christ spoke to
the Good Thief, "Today you will be with me in Paradise"
(Luke 23:43), then there are words no more terrifying than
those of this divine decree, "They shall not enter into my
rest." With what great anguish we should read in Sacred
Scripture and proclaim daily at our pre-dawn vigil how the
Hebrews "tested [God] and put [God] to the proof, though
they had seen [His] work" (Psalm 95:9). Having set before
them life and death, Moses exhorted the people to choose
life. But despite the mighty deeds which they had clearly

---

seen, they repeatedly chose death. Woefully conscious of their rebellious heritage, the Israelites' descendants in Babylonian exile lamented that "from the day when the Lord brought [their] fathers out of the land of Egypt until today, [they had] been disobedient to the Lord [their] God, and [they had] been negligent, in not heeding his voice" (Baruch 1:19).

Centuries later, echoing the refrain of Meriba and Massah, Christ rebuked Chorazin and Bethsaida for failing to repent after having witnessed the mighty deeds which He Himself had performed in their midst. The citizens of Chorazin and Bethsaida had eyes and ears, but they failed to see and hear. "And you, Capernaum," Jesus continued, "will you be exalted to heaven? You will be brought down to Hades" (Luke 10:15). For, lamentably, its inhabitants had also chosen death.

Every generation must confront for itself the perennial choice between life and death. Our generation is no exception. Like the Hebrew people at Meriba on the day of Massah, we ourselves stand before streams of life-giving water flowing forth from the Rock who is Christ (cf. 1 Corinthians 10:4). Our Savior compassionately invites us to draw water from His open Heart: "If anyone thirst, let him come to me and drink" (John 7:37). From Him flow the living waters which unfailingly quench man's thirst. Will we "draw water joyfully from the springs of salvation" (Preface for the Solemnity of the Sacred Heart, *The Roman Missal*, 3rd edition, 2011), or will we close our parched mouths to Christ? During these days of retreat, Christ pours forth His grace upon us. Are our hearts open to receive His gift?

In his Meditation on the Two Standards found in the Second Week of the *Spiritual Exercises*, Saint Ignatius presents us with the Mosaic choice in christological form (cf. IG-NATIUS OF LOYOLA, *Spiritual Exercises* § 136-148). Are we to be seduced by a love of money which leads to false honor and deadly pride and thus fall into line behind the banner of Satan as we march our way into hell? Or do we choose Christ? Do we choose to be poor with Christ poor, insulted with Christ loaded with insults, and thought the fool with Christ deemed hopelessly foolish? Do we choose to embrace the humility of the One "who, though he was in the form of God, did not count equality with God a thing to be grasped, but emptied himself, taking the form of a servant, being born in the likeness of men. And found in human form he humbled himself and became obedient unto death, even death on a cross" (Philippians 2:6-8)? Will we join the ranks of the Apostles, martyrs and saints who served under Christ's banner? Or will we pledge allegiance to Satan's standard? What will we choose? Life or death? Satan or Christ?

Each of us present in this chapel is similar in his own way to the Israelites at Meriba and the first-century Jews at Chorazin and Bethsaida inasmuch as we, too, have seen the mighty deeds of the Lord in our own lives. Had we not beheld God's providence or heard His voice at some graced moment, we simply would not be here today. My brothers, today is the day of Massah. We stand at the place of Meriba. From Christ's wounded side pierced by the soldier's lance flow streams of living water. At the altar we will witness with eyes of faith the mightiest of deeds before which winged seraphim veil the face: created elements gathered from field and vine become God's flesh and blood. Will you choose life, or will you choose death? Are you to be exalted to heaven or go down to the netherworld? Will you forsake God's rest or enter this day with Him into Paradise?

There is particular urgency in your present choice. For, a year from now—*Deo volente*—the Church will call you to Holy Orders. You will be ordained deacons and eventually priests to preach God's Word. You will be the heralds of Christ's Gospel. Therefore, my brothers, I exhort you to delay no longer. Set aside everything in your lives that is not of Christ. Choose Christ, serve under His banner, and live!

Rocca di Papa, 3 October 2003
Memorial of Saint Francis Borgia

II

ARMED WITH A TWO-EDGED SWORD
Believing, teaching and living the revealed Word of God

Reading: Proverbs 30: 5 – 9

In September 2004 the Dean of the theology faculty at the Gregorian University asked me if I would be his delegate to the archdiocesan seminary in the Cuban capital. Plans were underway for the seminary to enter into an affiliation with our faculty, and a delegate needed to be appointed. Was I willing, he inquired, to be our man in Havana? Confident that the good Lord always provides, I immediately agreed. This past June I visited Cuba for the third time. Every time that I have passed through the doors of the *Seminario de San Carlos y San Ambrosio*, a deep-seated joy has filled my heart.

My travels to Cuba have taught me much about the importance of ideas. A billboard on the road from the Havana airport into the city proclaims: *Las ideas son el arma esencial en la lucha de la humanidad* ("Ideas are the essential weapon in the fight of humanity.") I myself have experienced the occasional skirmish on the frontline of that crucial battle. Once when I was entering Cuba and then again on another occasion when I was exiting the country, my books and various papers were subject to examination. Take, for example, my departure from Havana this past June. While the airport security official expressed absolutely no concern that my carry-on luggage contained a razor, a small pair of scissors, more than three ounces of liquid soap and, yes, don't laugh, a bottle of shampoo, she demanded to know if I had a Bible in my suitcase. In my own defense I should point out that normally I would have checked that bag containing those items by now generally forbidden to be carried on board an airplane. But when I explained to the airlines' representative at the check-in counter what the bag contained, she assured me, "Padre, aquí no es problema." The bottle of water that I took through security was obviously not a problem, either. But my Bible apparently was. After I had surrendered the Good Book to the security agent, who thankfully later returned it, she fixed her eyes on my breviary and other papers. Potentially explosive liquids and sharp metal objects were thought to be harmless. But my Latin breviary and the Word of God proved too dangerous to be ignored.

Why does the Bible prove a threat? Quite simply because God's Word cuts more deeply than a two-edged sword. The security agent realized that perhaps better than many Christians. God's Word is the Truth which sets men free. For some, such liberating truth is indeed subversive.

At your diaconal ordination, which for most of you will take place—*Deo volente*—one year from now at the Altar of the Chair in Saint Peter's Basilica, you will solemnly receive the Word of God. Entrusting God's Word to you, the bishop will exhort you to believe what you read, to teach what you believe and to practice what you teach. He will arm you with the Word of God and call you to fidelity in its proclamation by word and deed for the salvation of souls. He will exhort you to communicate faithfully to others what you yourselves have received.

The *Book of Proverbs* calls us to a similar fidelity. It exhorts us to add nothing to God's words, lest He rebuke us and we be found to be liars. To add to God's Word effectively implies that we have found it to be wanting, that we are somehow dissatisfied with what we have received. So, we embellish it. We fabricate our own truth, that is, we lie. We conform God's teaching to our ways rather than our ways to His teaching. Thus we make ourselves the Word's masters rather than its servants. Yet the Church's Magisterium itself, to whom alone the task of authentically and authoritatively interpreting God's Word has been entrusted, "is not superior to the Word of God, but is its servant. It teaches only what has been handed on to it. At the divine command and with the help of the Holy Spirit, it listens to this devotedly, guards it with dedication and expounds it faithfully" (Vatican II, *Dei Verbum* § 10).

In order to avoid the divine rebuke which adding to God's Word merits, the oracle Agur, the son of Jakeh of Massa, asks two things of the Lord and pleads that they not be denied him before he dies: (1) that all falsehood and lying be removed from him, and (2) that he be given neither poverty nor riches. By his first request Agur rejects the falsification of God's Word through addition. In the spirit of the Church Fathers, I propose that Agur's second request likewise refers to the Word of God and complements the first.

In his second request, Agur desires nothing more than that the Lord "feed [him] with the food that is needful for [him]" (Proverbs 30:8). What is this necessary food, this daily bread, if not God's Word? For "man shall not live by bread alone, but by every word that proceeds from the mouth of God" (Matthew 4:4). Note, however, that Agur desires to be fed but not to be sated. For he fears a self-sufficiency in spiritual matters which would lead him to say, "Who is the Lord?" (Proverbs 30:9). He rightly fears making himself the Word's master who arrogantly adds to it rather than its servant who humbly receives it. The preacher should express similar concerns. For, his ordained mission is to preach Christ and God's Kingdom, not to preach himself and his own dominion.

Agur desires neither riches nor poverty. He would not add to God's Word thereby imposing himself upon it, nor would he subtract from God's Word thus disarming it. We subtract from God's Word when we fail to believe it. Our lack of faith impoverishes it—not, of course, in and of itself, but rather in our regard. By our disbelief, we lose our taste for its sweet savor. When we suffer such poverty, we can be easily tempted to turn to theft in order to satisfy our spiritual needs. We begin to look elsewhere for our spiritual nourishment—to pseudo-spiritualities or esoteric practices, to secular philosophies or purely mundane psychologies. We no longer live by the Word of God. The poverty of a preacher, who no longer believes the revealed Word of God, cannot be hidden. It will reveal itself in both his words and his deeds. His sermons will cease to inspire, and his life may soon begin to give scandal. He becomes salt which has lost its flavor, "no longer good for anything except to be thrown out and trodden underfoot by men" (Matthew 5:13).

During these days of retreat, the Lord Himself feeds you with His Word—the very Word which the bishop will exhort you to receive, read, believe, teach and live. Your faith-filled reception of God's Word begins now in the silence and solitude of these days, not in the glorious splendor of the ordination rite at the papal basilica on the Vatican hill. For, if it were only to begin there, it would not begin at all. In fact, my brothers, it began a long time ago. Had it not, you would not be here. Christ has nourished you with His Word for many years. In your future ministry, may you know neither the poverty nor the riches which Agur hoped to avoid. To that end, take to heart Saint Paul's instruction to Saint Timothy: "Preach the word, be urgent in season and out of season, convince, rebuke, and exhort, be unfailing in patience and in teaching. For the time is coming when people will not endure sound teaching, but having itching ears they will accumulate for themselves teachers to suit their own likings, and will turn away from listening to the truth and wander into myths. As for you, always be steady, endure suffering, do the work of an evangelist, fulfill your ministry" (2 Timothy 4:2-5).

During these spiritual exercises, you will meditate upon God's Word. Training you for *la lucha de la humanidad*, the Lord Himself arms you with a two-edged sword. Learn to wield it well.

Santa Marinella, 22 September 2010

27

III

THE CALL OF SAINT MATTHEW
Preaching the Gospel of Mercy according to Caravaggio

Reading: Ephesians 4:1-7, 11-13
Gospel: Matthew 9:9-13

Today the Church celebrates the feast of Saint Matthew, Apostle and Evangelist—a sinner called to be a companion of Jesus. The Gospel recounts his vocation story in stark terms. Jesus passes by, sees Matthew at the customs post, and says to him, "Follow me." Note carefully. We are told that Jesus sees Matthew, not that Matthew sees Jesus. Apparently, Matthew had not yet come to know of Jesus. He had not yet beheld Him among the crowds. He had not yet been intrigued by His preaching, drawn by His person and moved to become His disciple. No. In Matthew's case the initiative clearly belongs to Christ. Indeed, the initiative is always His, for it is He who has loved us first. Jesus sees Matthew thoroughly absorbed in his notorious occupation, seated at the customs post, collecting taxes. Jesus catches Matthew in the very act, as it were, and calls him, nonetheless. When Jesus calls Matthew, He does not call a man of exemplary virtue, but rather an as-of-yet unreformed sinner. He does not call an already well-trained spiritual athlete, but rather a tax collector—a man whom the self-righteous categorically despise. Christ looks upon Matthew with love, and it is His love for him which draws Matthew forth from his sin. Of Saint Matthew Christ can most truly say: "You did not choose me, but I chose you" (John 15:16).

Caravaggio's masterpiece *The Call of Saint Matthew*, which adorns the eastern wall of the chapel dedicated to the Evangelist in the Roman church of San Luigi dei Francesi, captures the precise moment of this dramatic encounter. With hand raised Christ points to Matthew. Caravaggio purposefully positions Christ's hand in the same posture which Michelangelo had portrayed the newly created Adam's outstretched hand in his own masterpiece on the Sistine Chapel ceiling. At San Luigi dei Francesi, Christ the New Adam calls Matthew in mercy and re-creates him in grace. Mirroring Christ on Caravaggio's canvas stands Saint Peter whose own hand is similarly outstretched. Christ's Vicar, a sinful man called to be a fisherman of men, collaborates with Christ in calling another as he himself had been called. Peter serves as apprentice to Christ in that nascent apostolic guild. According to the Caravaggian scene, Matthew is among the first of Saint Peter's newly collaborative catch. The tax collector as well will be helping the Lord soon enough to catch others like himself.

Seated at the customs table, Matthew looks up from the financial affairs at hand and gazes at Christ. Having heard the Lord call, he points to himself, and with an astonished look on his face, he seemingly says: "Who? Me?" Jesus, it appears, must be mistaken. Peter himself had previously thought as much when he knelt before Jesus amidst a massive catch of fish flopping about in his boat. "Depart from me," Peter had protested, "for I am a sinful man, O Lord" (Luke 5:8). But in neither case was Jesus to be deterred. Thankfully, Caravaggio's Matthew keeps his eyes squarely fixed upon Jesus and does not allow his gaze to wander to the chapel's western wall. Had he taken a quick glimpse at the ultimate cost of the discipleship to which Christ called him, he may never have gotten up from that customs table and followed Him. Had the neophyte-disciple seen his apostolic self slain by the sword, he would have had good cause to question the wisdom of answering such a call. For only the mature disciple grown to full stature in Christ can insist with Pauline conviction that neither tribulation, nor distress, nor persecution, nor famine, nor nakedness, nor peril, nor the sword can ever "separate us from the love of God in Christ Jesus our Lord" (Romans 8.39).

Longing to share a meal with Matthew, Jesus figuratively stands and knocks at the door of his heart (cf. Revelation 3:20). Fortified by grace Matthew gets up, opens the door and welcomes Him. In fact, Jesus does go soon afterwards to Matthew's house in order to dine with him. But Matthew and Jesus are not alone. Tax collectors and sinners join Jesus and His disciples at table. The self-righteous are appalled by the company which Christ keeps. But Christ the Physician reminds the allegedly healthy that He has come to minister to the sick. He has not come to call the righteous but sinners. In fact, He has come to call you and me.

Christ the Physician binds our wounds and heals our infirmities so that once renewed in His love and strengthened by His grace we can minister to others the mercy which we

31

ourselves have first received from Him. Through Christ Jesus, "the Father of mercies and God of all comfort … comforts us in all our afflictions, so that we may be able to comfort those who are in any affliction with the comfort with which we ourselves are comforted by God" (2 Corinthians 1:3-4). In this light Jesus calls us, His priests, from among sinners reconciled in His mercy and sends us forth as heralds of that same divine mercy to those in need. During the *Year for Priests*, Pope Benedict XVI noted the audacity of God to entrust the sacred priesthood to such earthen vessels, to such inescapably flawed instruments, to sinners such as ourselves called to be companions of Christ. If the priesthood were all about us, it would indeed have been a disastrous decision. But thankfully, the priesthood is not about us. It is rather all about Jesus and His mercy—Jesus in us and His mercy working through us. Paradoxically, our own struggles with sin enhance our mission of mercy. On this account, notes Saint Optatus of Milevis, a lesser known fourth-century North African Church Father, Christ gave the keys of the kingdom to the sinner Peter, in order that he open the gates of heaven to the innocent, and not to the innocent lest they close those gates against sinners (cf. OPTATUS OF MILEVIS, *Against the Donatists* 7.3.11-12).

We have received a tremendous call to follow Christ as His priests. Through our prayer and pastoral experience, Christ gently reveals to us everything that the priesthood entails—suffering and sacrifice having no little part to play in it. It seems unlikely that Matthew envisioned his martyrdom as he stood up from that customs table and left his sinful life behind. But the cross was nonetheless present from the start. The entire scene in Caravaggio's masterpiece unfolds underneath the sign of the cross depicted by the intersecting wooden beams supporting the glass panes of the room's only visible window. Similarly, the cross plays a crucial role in our own vocational discernment. It is not the absence of the cross, the absence of suffering, which confirms our sacerdotal vocation. For, there is no Christian vocation without the cross. Rather, it is the presence of joy—the joy with which we are able to bear the particular cross which Christ would have us bear. Thus sustained by joy we are confident "that the sufferings of this present time are not worth comparing with the glory that is to be revealed to us" (Romans 8:18). It was undoubtedly such joy in knowing Christ that drew the sinner Matthew forth and ultimately led him to shed his blood for the Merciful One whom he so dearly loved.

Between the initial moments of our own call and its final consummation in death, however, we rightly live our priestly lives in the scene of that middle canvas on the southern wall of the Saint Matthew chapel. There, Caravaggio depicts Saint Matthew writing his Gospel at the angel's prompting. The Evangelist records the Good News of our salvation. He extols the mercy of God—the very mercy which he himself had first experienced on the day that the Lord called. As priests we, too, are called to proclaim Christ's mercy and to minister it through the Sacraments to others. We do so most effectively when we begin by witnessing to the presence of Christ's mercy in our own lives, that is, when we share with others our own experience of being sinners reconciled in mercy and called by grace to be the companions of Christ.

Santa Marinella, 21 September 2011

33

IV

SAINT BRUNO
AND EVANGELICAL SIMPLICITY
Abandoning all things to follow Christ

Gospel: Mark 10:17-31

On two occasions your patron, Saint Bruno, success-fully avoided election to the episcopacy. After the deposition of the simoniac Archbishop of Rheims, Manasses of Gour-nay, in 1080, the clergy and people of Rheims intended to elect Bruno of Cologne as his successor. Bruno was already well known to them for his brilliant intellect and moral in-tegrity. For almost a quarter century, he had masterfully di-rected the renowned archdiocesan school of Rheims, also serving briefly towards the end of his tenure as the arch-diocesan chancellor. In this latter capacity, Bruno, along with other canons of the Cathedral Chapter, had resisted Arch-bishop Manasses's corrupt, oppressive leadership. On ac-count of his steadfast opposition, Bruno suffered exile and the confiscation of his material possessions. After the re-forming Pope, Saint Gregory VII, had definitively deposed the simoniac Archbishop, the clergy and people of Rheims turned to Bruno. But Bruno resisted their efforts to make him bishop, for sometime before he had vowed "to leave the fleeting shadows of the world to go in search of the good that is everlasting and receive the monastic habit" (BRUNO, *Letter to Raoul le Verd* 13 (SC 88.76)).

After an initial experience with Cistercian monasticism still in seminal form, Bruno journeyed to Grenoble. There he met the saintly Bishop Hugh who led Bruno and his six companions to the Chartreuse—an austere Alpine ravine hidden among the craggy mountains of the Dauphiné not far from Grenoble. Hardly accessible under the best of conditions, it proved an ideal location for an eremitical life of solitude, silence and contemplative prayer. The rugged terrain also assured the hermits a frugal life. Hidden away for six years in the shadowy recesses of the Chartreuse, Bruno lived his monastic ideal until the day when his former student, Pope Urban II, called his venerable teacher to Rome to serve as his counselor. Once again Bruno abandoned all things in order to follow Christ's call now made manifest in the summons of Christ's Vicar. Not long after Bruno's arrival in the Eternal City, he was obliged to follow the Roman Pontiff into Calabrian exile as the papal court fled before the hostile forces of the excommunicate German Emperor and his anti-pope.

At Reggio in Calabria, where the Apostle Saint Paul had first set foot on the Italian peninsula, the clergy, recently bereft of their bishop, soon elected Bruno as his successor. Yet Bruno again declined the episcopal miter and crosier. Free from all clerical ambition, he desired only one thing—the *unicum necessarium* which Mary of Bethany had enjoyed at the feet of Jesus. He desired to live a life of unencumbered contemplation. Unwilling to part completely with his saintly teacher, Pope Urban permitted Bruno to return to an eremitical life but this time in a secluded wooded valley nestled atop the Calabrian mountains. Bruno constructed his cell alongside a crystal-clear stream flowing briskly through the dense primeval forest. He dwelt there for the remaining decade of his life. Your class's diaconal ordination in Saint Peter's Basilica on October 6th will fall on the 910th anniversary of the saintly Carthusian's death.

As a class you have placed yourselves under Saint Bruno's patronage. To espouse a patron, especially a heavenly patron, is not an indifferent act. By such an act, one enters into a pact with him, both following his lead and benefitting from his support. So, what may you expect from Saint Bruno's patronage? Where is he most likely to lead you? His own path led him away from the fleeting shadows of the world—from all clerical ambition, material possessions and worldly success—into the simplicity, silence and solitude of a Carthusian cell. Ordained for service in the diocesan clergy, you will not live a life of monastic seclusion. But this does not mean that Saint Bruno's patronage is irrelevant to your vocation. On the contrary, he will counsel you as he once counseled a pope zealous for clerical reform. He will lead you along the path of the pure heart which sees God, the poverty of spirit which inherits the heavenly kingdom, and the austerity of a priestly life wholly consecrated to God's service. Bruno exemplifies the radical simplicity inherent in Christian discipleship and necessary for credible priestly witness. The call to such radical evangelical simplicity comes from Christ Jesus Himself. Saint Bruno, along with all the

JOSEPH CAROLA, SJ

saints from the Apostles to Blessed John Paul II[1], heard this
call. They left everything and followed Jesus in evangelical
simplicity. Baptism has set you firmly upon this humble
path—the *via dell'umiltà*. Sacred Orders will commit you to
walk even more fervently upon it.

Jesus' entire earthly life was a journey—a journey to
Calvary. As Jesus made His way to Jerusalem, He called others to join Him. The rich fellow in the Gospel, which we
have heard proclaimed, does not even wait to be summoned.
He runs up to Jesus and kneels before Him, asking the Good
Teacher what he must do to inherit eternal life. Jesus' immediate response may at first take us aback. "Why do you call
me good?", the Lord asks, "No one is good but God alone"
(Mark 10:18). An attentive reading of the text reveals that,
while Jesus questions the title's invocation, He does not deny
its application. Rather, Christ the Good Teacher rightly instructs that God alone is good—the source of all goodness.
"O Bonitas!", your patron Saint Bruno would often exclaim
when beholding God in all things. "What is more sound and
more beneficial, more innate, more in accord with human
nature than to love the good?" Saint Bruno asks a friend re-
luctant to fulfill a private vow made to God, "And what is as
good as God? Still more, is there anything good besides
God? So, the holy soul who has any comprehension of this
good, of his incomparable brilliance, splendor, and beauty,
burns with the flames of heavenly love and cries out: 'I thirst

---

[1] On 27 April 2014, Pope Francis canonized Pope John Paul II.

for God, the living God. When will I come and see the face of God?' (Psalm 42:3)" (BRUNO, *Letter to Raoul le Verd* 16 (SC 88.78)). In hailing Christ the Good Teacher, the rich fellow in the Gospel account thus proclaims Him divine. He effectively kneels in adoration before Him. Indeed, Christ's divinity alone can justify His all-encompassing demand: that the fellow abandon everything and follow Him in order to inherit eternal life. Jesus can make this demand because He Himself is the Way, the Truth and the Life, and no one comes to the Father except through Him (cf. John 14:6).

In answering the rich fellow's question, Christ the Good Teacher employs sound pedagogy. He starts with what is familiar. He begins with the Mosaic Law—a law which He has not come to abolish but rather to fulfill. "You know the commandments" (Mark 10:19), Jesus presumes. The fellow insists that he has observed them from his youth. He has lived a chaste, honest and obedient life. He is a virtuous man. He is an observant Jew. We do well to recall here that the Pharisee Saul had also been an observant Jew whom few if any could rival in knowledge of the Law and practice of its precepts (cf. Philippians 3:4-8). In a similar vein, Saint Bruno had long been known for his outstanding intellect and moral integrity. In each case the moral foundation was firmly laid. But Christian discipleship is not merely a matter of morals. One thing more is required—required of the rich fellow and indeed required of us all.

Before describing the demands of discipleship, Saint Mark relates a particular detail not found in the parallel synoptic accounts. The Evangelist observes that "Jesus looking upon [the rich fellow] loved him" (Mark 10:21). Christ's love frames the call. "In this is love," Saint John explains elsewhere, "not that we loved God but that he loved us and sent his Son to be the expiation for our sins" (1 John 4:10). Indeed, "we love, because he first loved us" (1 John 4:19). Christ's love for us enables our love for Him. The radical discipleship to which He calls us is only possible on account of His love graciously poured forth into our hearts. Christ's sacrificial love for us always precedes our sacrificial love for Him. In this vein Saint Paul reminds the Corinthians that Jesus "died for all, that those who live might live no longer for themselves but for him" (2 Corinthians 5:15).

In this loving context, the Good Teacher instructs the fellow kneeling before Him: "You lack one thing" (Mark 10:21). Indeed, as He once assured Martha in Mary's defense, only one thing is necessary. "Go," Jesus commands, "sell what you have, and give to the poor, and you will have treasure in heaven; and come, follow me" (Mark 10:21). Christ counsels those who would be His disciples to abandon all things and to follow Him in evangelical simplicity in order to inherit eternal life. Such simplicity entails both an internal detachment from material possessions and a concretely frugal manner of living. As Jesus preached on the Mount of the Beatitudes: "Blessed are the poor in spirit, for theirs is the kingdom of heaven" (Matthew 5:3). Indeed, "blessed are you poor" (Luke 6:20), according to the Lucan account. Christ exhorts us even today: "Do not lay up for yourselves treasures on earth ... but lay up for yourselves treasure in heaven. ... For where your treasure is, there will your heart be also" (Matthew 6:19-21). He warns us, furthermore: "You cannot serve God and mammon" (Matthew 6:24).

If we hope to inherit eternal life in the heavenly kingdom, then we should honestly ask ourselves: where is our treasure, where are our hearts, whom do we serve? Do not think that such radical simplicity is simply for the sons of Saint Bruno secluded in their Carthusian cells. Rather, Christ thus counsels all who would follow Him. If such radical simplicity pertains to the priesthood of all the baptized faithful, then how much more should it pertain to Christ's ordained ministers! Here the baptismal priesthood and the ministerial priesthood, which differ fundamentally in essence, also clearly differ in degree (cf. Vatican II, *Lumen Gentium* § 10). They differ in essence according to the manner of their distinct participations in Jesus' unique priesthood. For, while the baptismal priesthood does indeed fully participate in the one priesthood of Jesus Christ, the ordained priesthood uniquely participates in Christ's headship. In contrast to the baptismal priesthood, the ordained priest stands and ministers *in persona Christi capitis*. The Second Vatican Council's Dogmatic Constitution *Lumen Gentium*, however, further instructs that, while differing in essence, the baptismal and ministerial priesthoods also differ in degree. The call to evangelical simplicity among other dimensions characterizes this latter distinction. While all the Christian faithful are called to evangelical simplicity in order to inherit eternal life, Christ most especially calls the ordained through the Church to bear witness to their consecration—their total gift of self—by means of a truly frugal lifestyle which visibly proclaims to the baptized faithful and indeed to the entire world that their treasure is not on earth but in heaven. By his uncompromised evangelical simplicity, the *alter Christus caput* witnesses most credibly to the poor Christ crucified to whom he has been sacramentally conformed.

The chaste, honest and obedient fellow in the Gospel, who so deeply desires to inherit eternal life, is crestfallen at Jesus' answer. "At that saying," Saint Mark relates, "his countenance fell, and he went away sorrowful; for he had great possessions" (Mark 10:22). These are tremendous words which should fill all who hear them with fear and trembling. This virtuous man abandons Christ rather than his numerous possessions. "What is more perverse," your patron Saint Bruno asks, "more contrary to reason, to justice, and to nature itself, than to prefer creature to Creator, to pursue perishable goods instead of eternal ones, those of earth rather than those of heaven" (BRUNO, *Letter to Raoul le Verd* 8 (SC 88.72))? How different the rich man's response is from that of Saint Paul who according to his own reckoning was not only similarly blameless, but indeed practically unparalleled in righteousness under the Law (cf. Philippians 3:6). "I count everything as loss," the Apostle writes to the Philippians, "because of the surpassing worth of knowing Christ Jesus my Lord. For his sake I have suffered the loss of all things, and count them as refuse, in order that I may gain Christ" (Philippians 3:8). Saint Paul abandoned all things in order to follow Christ. The Apostle sets the standard for priestly ministry carried out in evangelical simplicity. Imitating Saint Paul we priests should "put no obstacle in anyone's way so that no fault may be found with our ministry, but as servants of God we commend ourselves in every way: ... as poor, yet making many rich; as having nothing, and yet possessing everything" (2 Corinthians 6:3-4,10).

At the rich man's departure, Christ the Good Teacher does not conclude His lesson. Rather, He turns His attention to those who have already committed themselves to journeying with Him to Jerusalem, and He sets about to uproot from their hearts any possible lingering allurement posed by a so-called prosperity gospel. "How hard it will be for those who have riches to enter the kingdom of God" (Mark 10:23), Jesus proclaims twice to their utter amazement. Can no one then be saved, the dumbfounded disciples ask, effectively implying that God's blessing, material well-being and eternal life go hand-in-hand. Moving quickly to squelch all proto-Pelagian tendencies among His followers, Jesus asserts that naked human industry and eternal salvation enjoy no causal relationship. Assessing the sacrifices already undertaken for Jesus' sake, Peter exclaims in exasperation: "Lo, we have left everything and followed you" (Mark 10:28). Peter's impassioned plea seemingly suggests that his initial motives for following Christ were not completely pure. Did he seek first the Kingdom *in order that* all other material things might be his as well (cf. Matthew 6:33)? Indeed, soon enough James and John to the consternation of their companions will ask to sit at Jesus' right and left in glory—a glory still envisioned in earthly terms. If anything, in this apostolic aula, Jesus the Good Teacher has ample opportunity to practice Carthusian patience!

The Lord immediately allays his disciples' fears. He assures them that the abandonment of property and familial relationships for His sake and the Gospel's will not go unrewarded. Yes, His disciples will receive the hundredfold even in this life—but a hundredfold tempered by persecutions. In other words, the hundredfold of love and grace, which they shall enjoy in this life, and the eternal life, which awaits them in the age to come, are the fruits of the Cross, and the Cross entails a stripping bare. Jesus most certainly does not preach a so-called prosperity gospel. Rather, the Good Teacher instructs His disciples that in order to inherit eternal life they must ascend Calvary, be stripped of all things and conformed to Him Crucified. The one thing which the rich fellow lacks is the Cross, and it is the one thing that he refuses to embrace. By his refusal, he, who is among the first in virtue, risks being found on Judgment Day among the last.

The Gospel reveals that Christ calls all who would be His disciples to follow Him in simplicity. On this account, evangelical simplicity is not merely the luxury of vowed Religious. Rather their consecrated poverty serves to rivet the attention of all the Christian faithful to Christ's universal call. The diocesan clergy are certainly not exempt. On the contrary! Calling priests to both an internal detachment from and a proper stewardship of earthly goods, the Second Vatican Council likewise invites priests "to embrace voluntary poverty by which they are more manifestly conformed to Christ and become eager in the sacred ministry" (Vatican II, *Presbyterorum Ordinis* § 17). The council fathers continue that priests "should avoid everything which in any way could turn the poor away. Before the other followers of Christ, let priests set aside every appearance of vanity in their possessions" (Ibid.). The Church's canon law codifies the conciliar decree, legislating that "clerics are to foster simplicity of life and are to refrain from all things that have a resemblance of vanity" (*Code of Canon Law* 282 § 1). Through the Church

Christ clearly calls priests to a life of exemplary evangelical simplicity.

At your diaconal ordination you will promise celibacy for the sake of the Kingdom and obedience to your Ordinaries. Who among you would think to place conditions on either promise? But at your diaconal ordination, you will also promise to discharge the office of deacon with humility and love and to shape your way of life always according to the example of Christ. Are you equally ready then to embrace wholeheartedly a life of evangelical simplicity and material frugality which avoids all semblance of vanity? Recall that, when the rich fellow approached Jesus, he had lived from his youth a chaste, honest and obedient life. It was neither a lack of chastity nor a lack of obedience, but rather his many possessions which impeded him from shaping his life according to the example of Christ. Of course, in your ordained ministry, you will legitimately make use of various earthly goods. You will need adequate housing, a decent bed, durable clothing, a suitable library, a dependable automobile, a reliable computer and by now a handy cell-phone. These will be among the tools of your trade. Even Saint Bruno and the first Carthusians had a fine library at the Chartreuse in order to aid their prayer and to support their work of copying manuscripts. In addition to material goods, you will also have a right to periodic rest and relaxation in order to return refreshed to your apostolic labors. But you must continually discern the extent to which such goods and recreation either aid or hinder your Christian discipleship and ordained ministry.

If one day more gold hangs about your neck and adorns your wrists and fingers than plates the chalice in your hands, you can be certain that something has gone awry. If you dine more sumptuously, dress more luxuriously and recreate more lavishly than the average family in your parish, something is definitely wrong. If such were ever to occur, pray fervently to hear anew Christ's call to abandon all in order to follow Him, realizing as well that discerning the call to evangelical simplicity is not merely a matter of taking stock of one's material possessions. While it will concretely entail such an inventory, it is first and foremost about entering into Christ's love for us and our love for Him. Only then, faithful to the evangelical order which Saint Mark recounts, can we clearly hear Christ call us to journey with Him to Calvary in order to share in the victory of His Resurrection. Only then will we respond unreservedly to His observation that we lack one thing. For, our response will be made in love. In this light alone will we come to "count everything as loss because of the surpassing worth of knowing Christ Jesus [our] Lord" (Philippians 3:8). For, no material possession can ever compare to the love that Christ bears for us. When we love Him in return, no sacrifice will be too great for us to bear for Him.

In Saint Peter's Basilica stands Saint Bruno's statue. He reels back before a miter and crosier and clings to a skull, disciplinary chain and book. He symbolically embraces an ascetical life and the legitimate tools of his trade as he retreats before the risks which high ecclesiastical office cannot completely avoid. As archdiocesan chancellor Bruno opposed financial corruption among the clergy. Leaving "the fleeting shadows of the world to go in search of the good that is everlasting," he journeyed with Jesus to the Calvary of the Chartreuse and Calabria. In an extraordinary manner he models the call to evangelical simplicity inherent in Christian discipleship and especially necessary for Christ's ordained ministers. As members of the diocesan clergy, you will not follow your patron into the physical solitude of a Carthusian cell. But as you labor in the world for the salvation of souls, may you seek no less than Saint Bruno did the *unicum necessarium*. May you love Jesus without reserve. May you hear His call to abandon all things and to follow Him. May you know in this life the hundredfold of His love and His grace, and in the age to come may you through His mercy inherit eternal life.

Vatican City, 17 May 2011

47

V

CHRIST JESUS THE CELIBATE HIGH PRIEST
Loving our neighbor as Christ Jesus has loved us from
the Cross

Gospel: John 15:12-17

On the night of His passion, Jesus gave to His disciples
gathered in the Cenacle a new commandment: that we
should love one another as He has loved us. This new commandment of love in imitation of Christ pertains to all the
baptized faithful. Yet it would not be wrong to suggest that
it applies in a particular way to the ministerial priesthood and
even more so to those in both the Christian East and West
who live their priesthood in consecrated celibacy. While acknowledging the universal significance of the Johannine text,
I wish to explore with you one particular facet of its manifold spiritual depth: how this Gospel speaks to the heart of
the celibate priest.

Before we turn our attention to the content of Jesus'
final discourse, we should note its immediate context. Jesus
has gathered with His disciples in the Upper Room. He has
humbled Himself before them, washing their feet—washing

even the feet of the friend who would deny Him and of the one who would betray Him. At that Last Supper with His disciples, Jesus has instituted the Eucharist as the memorial of His passion, death and Resurrection. He has likewise instituted the priesthood for its faithful celebration throughout the ages until He comes again. At that first Eucharist He has offered the *sacramentum* of His Body and Blood whose *res* will be revealed upon the Cross before the sun sets again. This historical context is one of profound mystery—the redemptive mystery of sacrificial love sacramentally rendered present by Christ the celibate High Priest. This Paschal Mystery sheds evangelical light upon that intimate bond which for centuries has united the priesthood and consecrated celibacy.

At the heart of Jesus' final discourse lies His new commandment that we love one another as He has loved us. The twofold commandment of love which summarizes the Law and the Prophets was already known. We are to love God with our entire being and our neighbor as we love ourselves. But Jesus commands us further. He commands that in loving our neighbor we are to imitate His love for us. How has Jesus loved us? Jesus has loved us with a virginal love, a chaste love, a celibate love, a totally self-sacrificing love which engenders life—indeed, eternal life—within us. In a particular way, then, Jesus' new commandment calls the unmarried priest to incarnate in his own being Christ's celibate love so that by means of his celibacy the priest himself may become an iconic fulfillment of Christ's new commandment.

This priestly iconic conformity to Christ is the fruit of grace. Firstly, it is the fruit of sacramental grace. In Holy Orders a man is conformed in the very depths of his being to Christ the Head. He becomes an *alter Christus caput.* He stands and ministers *in persona Christi capitis.* Secondly, although consecrated celibacy is not a sacramental grace, it is nonetheless a supernatural gift given by Christ and freely embraced by the cleric "for the sake of the kingdom of heaven" (Matthew 19:12). This grace alone makes our Christ-like celibate love possible. For, we priests and those called to the priesthood know only all too well how easily lust, anger and disordered affections can invade our hearts, divide our wills and corrupt our love. Humbly we confess that every priest "chosen from among men ... is beset with weakness. Because of this he is bound to offer sacrifice for his own sins as well as for those of the people" (Hebrews 5:1-3). Yet, despite our human frailty and our sins, we are called to love others as Christ has loved us, and He has loved us with a pure, undivided and sinless Heart. Our hope, then, to love in imitation of Christ resides not in any self-acquired purity of our own, but rather in the pure love which Jesus Himself pours forth into our hearts (cf. Romans 5:5). In other words, to quote Saint John, "[w]e love, because he first loved us" (1 John 4:19). In this same vein Jesus reassures the celibate cleric: "You did not choose me, but I chose you" (John 15:16). Jesus has chosen us to be His priests, and He calls us to live our priesthood in consecrated celibacy, not only commanding us to love as He has loved us, but also giving us the grace to fulfill what He commands.

After revealing His new commandment to those gathered in the Upper Room, Jesus instructed them further: "Greater love has no man than this, that a man lay down his life for his friends" (John 15:13). What Jesus taught that night by His words He fulfilled the following day by His deeds. He laid down His life upon the Cross for us. In imitation of Christ, then, the celibate cleric also lays down his life in offering his own body "as a living sacrifice, holy and acceptable to God" (Romans 12:1). He is not conformed to the world around him, but rather through Holy Orders he has been sacramentally conformed to Christ Crucified. The gift of consecrated celibacy becomes the privileged prism through which the light of his sacramental conformity to the Crucified Christ shines forth and is refracted in its manifold splendor. In this refracted light, the words of Eucharistic institution reveal their depth of meaning in the priest's own person: "This is my Body which is given for you" (Luke 22:19). By means of his consecrated celibacy, the priest has "crucified [his] flesh with its passions and desires" (Galatians 5:24). With arms outstretched and nailed to the Cross, he selflessly embraces those whom he serves, sacrificing the physical, life-giving embrace of spouses in order to enfold with a spiritual embrace the entire world. By means of his celibacy, the priest witnesses in this life to that celestial life where "in the resurrection [men and women] neither marry nor are given in marriage, but are like angels in heaven" (Matthew 22:30).

In refracting the sacramental light of Holy Orders, the prism of consecrated celibacy especially reveals the conformity of the priest's heart to the Sacred Heart of Jesus. Like Christ, the celibate priest loves with a pierced heart. His heart is continually ripped open by Longinus' spear, dying to its natural and legitimate desires for the sake of a greater love.

This dying to self is indeed an intimate share in Christ's passion, and like Christ's passion it is a dying which bears fruit in abundant life. The celibate suffers this bittersweet piercing because he recognizes that it enables him to love all the more. Longinus' spear rips his heart open in order to expand it, continually enabling the celibate to welcome others into his heart without fear of ever displacing those who already abide therein. Indeed, the celibate's pierced heart loves most generously, knowing no limit in its affective outpouring.

Upon the Cross, Jesus the Good Shepherd laid down His life for His friends. We are His friends, Jesus assures us, if we do what He commands us (cf. John 15:14). But is it not the duty of a servant rather than the role of a friend to obey commands? How does obeying His commands make us anything more than mere servants? According to Our Lord's definition in the Johannine text, what distinguishes friendship from servitude is not the absence of commands. No, the distinction lies elsewhere. Knowledge—or, rather, its absence—is the distinguishing factor. Servants are not privy to their master's intentions. They obey in ignorance, simply executing orders and nothing more. Friends, on the other hand, enjoy a self-revelatory intimacy with one another. This intimate knowledge informs their mutual love. As Jesus explains: "No longer do I call you servants, for the servant does not know what his master is doing; but I have called you friends, for all that I have heard from my Father I have made known to you" (John 15:15). To shed further light upon this passage, let us momentarily turn our attention to the eleventh chapter of Saint Matthew's Gospel with its unmistakably Johannine overtones. "All things have been delivered to me by my Father;" Jesus instructs, "and no one knows the Son except the Father, and no one knows the Father except the Son and anyone to whom the Son chooses to reveal him" (Matthew 11:27). Those to whom Jesus reveals the Father are, as we know from Saint John's Gospel, Jesus' friends. So, then, it is His friends whom Our Lord subsequently commands: "Come to me, all who labor and are heavy laden, and I will give you rest. Take my yoke upon you, and learn from me; for I am gentle and lowly in heart, and you will find rest for your souls. For my yoke is easy, and my burden is light" (Matthew 11:28-30). What is this easy yoke and light burden if not the new commandment which Jesus has given to us: to love one another as He has loved us? The celibate cleric fulfills this commandment by laying down his life as Christ did upon the Cross. This commandment is made easy and light because, as we have already noted, Christ pours forth His own chaste love into our hearts so that we may love as He has loved us.

In this evangelical light the universal obligation of celibacy for Catholic priests of the Latin Rite is properly understood. Yes, it is a discipline. But it is, in fact, much more. For it is not simply a matter of servitude, of ignorantly bearing an external burden imposed upon us by another. It is not a matter of a command mindlessly if not even begrudgingly executed. Rather, it is the call of Christ the Friend who invites us into the depths of His own Heart where He reveals to us the Father's boundless love. There *cor ad cor loquitur*— heart speaks to heart. There we enter into an intimate friendship with Christ. What was once said of Jonathan and David can be said of us and Jesus: "…the soul of Jonathan was knit to the soul of David, and Jonathan loved him as his own soul" (1 Samuel 18:1). In this most intimate friendship, our hearts and the Heart of Christ become as one. Our priestly celibate love becomes an authentic reflection of Christ's love in the world. Like the new commandment, then, the promise of celibacy defines our sacerdotal friendship with Christ Jesus.

Our celibacy is faithfully lived within this context of friendship—first and foremost in friendship with Christ sustained through the Sacraments and prayer, but also in friendship with our fellow priests who are the Lord's own intimate friends as well as in friendship with those whom we selflessly serve. Indeed, by no means is celibacy a matter of foregoing friendship. On the contrary, as the Scriptures most powerfully reveal, it is a matter of entering intimately into friendship. "A faithful friend," we read in the *Book of Sirach*, "is a sturdy shelter: he that has found one has found a treasure" (Sirach 6:14). Good friends are that sturdy shelter wherein the priest faithfully lives his consecrated celibacy. Such good friends, for example, sustain the celibate in those moments of trial when he experiences more acutely that loneliness which no man, whether he be celibate or not, cannot completely avoid in this life of pilgrimage. In those periods of loneliness, we must especially turn in prayer to Christ our Friend. Alluding directly to the fifteenth chapter of Saint John's Gospel, Venerable Pope Paul VI[1] counsels further:

---

[1] On 19 October 2014, Pope Francis beatified Pope Paul VI.

[I]f hostility, lack of confidence and the indifference of his fellow men make his solitude quite painful, [the celibate cleric] will thus be able to share, with dramatic clarity, the very experience of Christ, as an apostle who must not be 'greater than he who sent him', as a friend admitted to the most painful and most glorious secret of his divine Friend who has chosen him to bring forth the mysterious fruit of life in his own life, which is only apparently one of death (POPE PAUL VI, *Sacerdotalis Caelibatus* § 59).

Jesus is no fair-weather friend, nor should we be. To suffer faithfully with Christ our Friend in such moments of painful solitude reveals the true mettle of our friendship.

Christ has chosen us to be His priests and to live our priesthood in consecrated celibacy. "Come to me," he lovingly commands, "Take my yoke upon you" (cf. Matthew 11:28-29). He commissions us and instructs "that [we] should go and bear fruit and that [our] fruit should abide" (John 15:16). We are called in imitation of Christ to generate life in others by means of our celibate love. It is the call of spiritual paternity, a fructifying celibacy. It is a call to generosity in our apostolic service. It is a call to live our celibacy always open to life. On this account even the celibate cleric must be wary of falling into a contraceptive mentality. A contracepting cleric, as it were, regrettably lives his celibacy closed to the generation of life in others. He avoids the sacrifice of himself in their service all the while seeking pleasures for himself in material things which while not violating his celibacy nonetheless turn his heart away from Christ. His celibate love loses its outward apostolic focus and egotistically turns within. He refuses to allow his heart to be pierced and ripped open so that others may enter in. This contraceptive mentality among celibate clerics is an abuse and indeed a failure in celibacy. For, the cleric's consecrated celibacy when authentically lived is anything but selfish and sterile. Rather it is a freely offered, sacrificial gift of self which generates life in those whom the celibate cleric serves. Christ has chosen and appointed us to shepherd His people and through laying down our lives in consecrated celibacy to bear fruit that will last "so that whatever [we] ask the Father in [His] name, he may give it to [us]" (John 15.16).

I have meant for my words to be consoling. By them I have sought to edify, to build you up, to strengthen you in the call which is yours as well as mine. For, the Cross, which is truly a cross, can be born faithfully only with joy. Otherwise, it cripples. But celibacy authentically lived is anything but crippling. It is liberating and life-giving for both the celibate and those whom he serves. In order to bear joyfully the life-giving cross of priestly celibacy, we must have constant recourse in prayer and through the Sacraments to Christ our Friend. Whenever we might stumble or, God forbid, if we should fall along our celibate path, let us turn immediately to Christ in the Sacrament of Penance. Let us implore Him, who did not hesitate to wash the feet of the one who denied Him as well as the one who betrayed Him, to wash our own feet. Indeed, our celibacy should always be lived in the Cenacle where Christ continually bathes us in His mercy. There in that Eucharistic context, we behold most clearly the intimate bond which unites our consecrated celibacy and the priesthood. There we celebrate that self-sacrificing love than which no greater exists. There Christ commands us to love in consecrated celibacy as He Himself has loved us. There He gives us the grace to fulfill joyfully what He commands, and in its fulfillment He embraces us as His friends.

Vatican City, 22 April 2013
Mary, Queen and Mother of the Society of Jesus

VI

SAINT MARTHA AND SAINT MARY
Magnanimously serving the Lord

Gospel: Luke 10:38-42

At Bethany a woman named Martha welcomed Jesus into her home. As she attended to the immediate demands of hospitality, her sister Mary "sat at the Lord's feet and listened to his teaching" (Luke 10:39). The Church counts both sisters among her saints. For, in welcoming the Lord into their home, they also welcomed Him into their hearts. They equally enjoyed Jesus' friendship. Yet, at this their first encounter with the Lord, one thing notably distinguishes them. In contrast to her sister Martha, Mary not only receives the Lord, but she also docilely receives from Him. What accounts for this difference?

Saint Luke explains that "Martha was distracted with much serving" (Luke 10:40). Although welcoming of the Lord and, no doubt, like her sister Mary, also fundamentally open to receiving from Him, Martha was distracted from receiving the good which the Lord Himself had to offer her because she was taken here and there by *much* serving. That

Martha serves the Lord is not the problem. For, indeed, men and women have been created in order to praise, reverence and serve God our Lord and by this graced means to attain to their salvation (cf. IGNATIUS OF LOYOLA, *Spiritual Exercises* § 23). "But Martha was distracted with much serving" (Luke 10:40). Her zealous service clearly overwhelmed her. She was overly solicitous about too many things—all good things, beyond doubt, done in the Lord's service, but quite simply too many things. Martha's unquestionably generous service lacked proper focus. She was overextended and stretched too thin. Ironically, distracted by so much service, Martha risked losing sight of the very One whom she so eagerly strove to serve.

Overwhelmed by the demands of hospitality, Martha complained to Jesus: "Lord, do you not care that my sister has left me to serve alone? Tell her to help me" (Luke 10:40). If, interpreting this passage spiritually, we take Martha as a symbol of the apostolic life dedicated to pastoral service, then her complaint is well taken. For, pastoral ministry unaccompanied by the contemplative life of prayer, which Mary symbolizes, all too easily loses sight of the Lord. When we lose sight of the Lord, we lose sight of the goal towards which our pastoral labors tend. Thus we, like Martha, become distracted by much serving. Our service becomes unfocused and undisciplined. Such unreflective service can easily overwhelm us and undermine our pastoral ministry. On this account, during his last Angelus on 24 February 2013, Pope Benedict XVI insisted upon "the primacy of prayer, without which the entire commitment to the apostolate and to charity is reduced to activism."[1] Such spiritually deficient, frenzied activism effectively reduces the minister to a mere machine and lamentably leads the Lord's servant away from the very Lord whom he hopes to serve. In this light, Martha rightly demands that Mary not leave her to serve alone. For, prayerful contemplation uniquely keeps our gaze fixed upon the One whom we serve.

Returning to the Scriptural text's dramatic action, we read that the Lord responded to Martha's complaint with a rebuke: "Martha, Martha, you are anxious and troubled about many things; one thing is needed" (Luke 10:41-42a). We should carefully note that Jesus does not rebuke Martha for attending to the demands of hospitality. It is right and just to serve the Lord. What the good Lord rebukes in Martha is the anxiety which torments her heart. Martha's anxiety betrays a lack of freedom in her service of the Lord. Troubled by many things, Martha lacks the ability to discern the greater good among the many goods to be done and to dedicate herself tranquilly to it. Consequently, she strives to do everything indiscriminately, which is impossible. In her undiscerning attempt to do more and more, she falls prey to an anxiety which binds her interiorly in a way that the Lord Himself never intended. What is the cause of this anxiety? What spirit moves Martha's heart?

---

[1] BENEDICT XVI, Sunday Angelus, 24 February 2013: http://www.vatican.va/holy_father/benedict_xvi/angelus/2013/documents/hf_ben-xvi_ang_20130224_en.html.

In his *Spiritual Exercises* Saint Ignatius of Loyola provides two sets of rules for the discernment of spirits. The first set is particularly suited for the First Week of the *Spiritual Exercises* during which the retreatant meditates upon his sins and the good Lord's boundless mercy. The second set of rules is more suitable for the Second Week of the *Spiritual Exercises* during which the retreatant contemplates Our Lord's infancy and public ministry. In the first set of rules, Saint Ignatius instructs that for those, who "earnestly [strive] to cleanse their souls from sin and who seek to rise in the service of God our Lord to greater perfection, ... it is characteristic of the evil spirit to harass with anxiety" (IGNATIUS OF LOYOLA, *Spiritual Exercises* § 315).[2] Accordingly, Martha's anxiety comes from the evil spirit who would impede her service and "prevent [her] soul from advancing" (Ibid.). We should note that the Evil One does not tempt her by what is obviously evil. Rather, he tempts her by what, in fact, is good. He manipulates her laudable desire to be generous in the Lord's service. Such temptation to the good is one of Satan's most subtle snares. Saint Ignatius unmasks this particularly clever, diabolic plot in his second set of rules for the discernment of spirits. "It is a mark of the evil spirit," the Jesuit Founder wisely counsels,

> to assume the appearance of an angel of light. He begins by suggesting thoughts that are suited to a devout

---

[2] IGNATIUS OF LOYOLA, *Spiritual Exercises*, trans. LOUIS J. PUHL, S.J. (Chicago: Loyola University Press, 1951), p. 141.

SAINT MARTHA AND SAINT MARY

soul, and ends by suggesting his own. For example, he will suggest holy and pious thoughts that are wholly in conformity with the sanctity of the soul. Afterwards, he will endeavor little by little to end by drawing the soul into his hidden snares and evil designs (*Spiritual Exercises* § 332).[3]

To remedy this ill, Saint Ignatius prescribes that we be constantly vigilant. We should examine our thoughts to be sure that they not only begin well, but that they also end well. For, "the course of thoughts suggested to us," Saint Ignatius warns,

> may terminate in something evil, or distracting, or less good than the soul had formerly proposed to do. Again, it may end in what weakens the soul, or disquiets it; or by destroying the peace, tranquility, and quiet which it had before, it may cause disturbance to the soul. These things are a clear sign that the thoughts are proceeding from the evil spirit, the enemy of our progress and eternal salvation (*Spiritual Exercises* § 333).[4]

Saint Ignatius's profound insights into the spiritual life serve to enhance our understanding of the Lord's rebuke in response to Martha's complaint.

As we have noted, the Lord does not rebuke Martha for her hospitality. To serve the Lord is a good thing—in-

---

[3] Ibid., p. 148.
[4] Ibid.

deed, a very good thing. For, by graciously and lovingly serving the Lord, we attain to our salvation. In fact, the Lord does not so much rebuke Martha as He does the evil spirit who causes her such intense anxiety. Ever so subtly Satan has managed to tempt this saintly woman by the holy thought of service wholly in conformity with the sanctity of her soul. But by drawing her into excessive service, he has succeeded in distracting her away from the Lord whom she strives to serve. The Evil One has disquieted her soul and destroyed her peace. In the name of the Lord's service, he has enticed her away from the *unicum necessarium*, the only thing truly necessary: the loving contemplation of the Lord which animates pastorally effective service. "One thing is needful," Jesus tells Martha, "Mary has chosen the good portion, which shall not be taken away from her" (Luke 10:42).

The Lucan account of the hospitality offered at Bethany not only demonstrates the traditional distinction between the contemplative and the active life, but it also addresses the virtue of magnanimity. In terms of magnanimity, Mary succeeded where Martha failed. Martha was distracted with much serving. She was anxious and troubled about many things. She lacked magnanimity. For, as Saint Thomas Aquinas drawing upon Aristotle's *Nicomachean Ethics* explains:

> The magnanimous person is said to be tranquil and leisurely, not because he is not solicitous about anything, but because he is not over-anxious about many things, but is confident and unworried over matters where he

ought to have trust. Too much fear and distrust make for excessive solicitude.[5]

While Martha succumbed to anxiety, Mary discerned the greater good among the many goods to be done, and she tranquilly dedicated herself to it. Mary exemplifies the magnanimous person who is "a man of few deeds, but of great and notable ones."[6] In his commentary on Aristotle's *Nicomachean Ethics*, Saint Thomas notes that the magnanimous person is both leisurely (*otiosus*) and slow (*tardus*) because he is neither engaged in many things nor does he easily involve himself in them.[7] He is not, however, lazy. For, he is, in fact, a generous benefactor prompt to do good for others as well as a contemplative more solicitous for the truth rather than human opinion.[8] His generous service brings him no anxiety because he has successfully integrated it into a properly ordered life. His is a disciplined life dedicated to fewer but greater things which are interior goods rather than external ones.[9] For him less is definitely more

---

[5] THOMAS AQUINAS, *Summa Theologiae* II-II, 47, 9, reply 3, vol. 36, trans. THOMAS GILBY, O.P. (Cambridge: Cambridge University Press, 2006), p. 31.

[6] ARISTOTLE, *Nichomachean Ethics* 1124^{b}25-26, *The Complete Works of Aristotle*, vol. 2, ed. JONATHAN BARNES (Princeton: Princeton University Press, 1984), p. 1775.

[7] Cf. THOMAS AQUINAS, *In Decem Libros Ethicorum Aristotelis ad Nicomachum Expositio* § 771.

[8] Cf. Ibid., § 773-774.

[9] Cf. Ibid., § 777.

and, indeed, better.[10] A virtuous mean orders his life. In his generous service he is neither timid nor foolhardy, but rather truly courageous, always discerning the greater good and never fearing, should it be necessary, even to lay down his life for the truly great without which life itself would not be worth living.[11] In other words, he neither fears martyrdom, nor does he risk his life unduly. Among the truly great things, for which the magnanimous person would ultimately be willing to die, Saint Thomas identifies the common good, justice and divine worship.[12] The latter is the better portion which Mary chose at Bethany. Sitting at Our Lord's feet and listening to His teaching, she magnanimously dedicated herself to the worship of God.

In order to serve magnanimously, one must proceed prudently—that is, one must properly discern the greater good to be done. The virtue of prudence is "right reason applied to action" (THOMAS AQUINAS, *Summa Theologiae* (*ST*) II-II, 47, 2, ad contra),[13] entailing the "rectitude of counsel, judgment and command" (*ST* II-II, 49, 6, reply 3). Firstly, it

---

[10] For a contemporary, immediately accessible elaboration of the classical understanding of magnanimity and prudence, cf. GREG MCKEOWN, *Essentialism: The Disciplined Pursuit of Less* (New York: Crown Business, 2014). While the book addresses the business world, it is widely applicable.

[11] Cf. ARISTOTLE, *Nichomachean Ethics* 1124^{b}7-10, p. 1774.

[12] Cf. THOMAS AQUINAS, *In Decem Libros Ethicorum Aristotelis ad Nicomachum Expositio* § 760.

[13] THOMAS AQUINAS, *Summa Theologiae* II-II, 1-148, vol. 3 (Westminster: Christian Classics, 1948).

SAINT MARTHA AND SAINT MARY

involves making inquiries, seeking advice and taking counsel. By this process, the prudent person proves himself to be a docile person who gradually acquires the natural virtue of prudence. He honestly recognizes that he "stands in very great need of being taught by others especially by old folk who have acquired a sane understanding of the ends in practical matters" (*ST* II-II, 49, 3, respondeo). Secondly, prudence entails making decisions. Once inquiries have been humbly made and information gathered, the prudent person judges the right course of action to be undertaken. The immediate fruit of his discernment is a well-informed decision. Thirdly and finally, the prudent person chooses. He acts upon his decision. He "appl[ies] to action the things counseled and judged" (*ST* II-II, 47, 8, respondeo). Hence, the prudent person is chiefly a man of action. He humbly discerns, wisely decides and decisively acts in a way most conducive to achieve his end.

Prudence, therefore, properly considers the means to an end and duly orders those means to that end (cf. *ST* II-II, 49, 6, respondeo). True and perfect prudence is ordered to the good end of one's entire life (cf. *ST* II-II, 47, 13, respondeo). What is this all-encompassing end? "Man is created," Saint Ignatius instructs, "to praise, reverence, and serve God our Lord and by this means to save his soul" (*Spiritual Exercises* § 23). All other things on earth have been created to aid men and women to attain this salvific end. The extent to which created goods aid us we make use of them, Saint Ignatius explains, but we are to set them aside if they prove a hindrance. Saint Ignatius' indifferent man is none other than Saint Thomas' "prudent man who considers things afar off, in so far as they tend to be a help or a hindrance to that which has to be done at the present time" (*ST* II-II, 47, 1, reply 2). This Thomistically prudent, Ignatianly indifferent man realizes that "it happens that a thing is good in itself and suitable to the end, and nevertheless becomes evil or unsuitable to the end, by reason of some combination of circumstances" (*ST* II-II, 49, 7, respondeo). In other words, he is alert to those Second-Week temptations towards the good which we identified earlier—temptations to which generous individuals like Martha are particularly susceptible. On this account, the prudent person proceeds cautiously not because he is excessively timid or indecisive, but rather because he is thoroughly aware of the subtleties involved in making a good decision and acting decisively upon it. "Even as false is found with true," Saint Thomas observes, "so is evil mingled with good [in contingent matters of action], on account of the great variety of these matters of action, wherein good is often hindered by evil, and evil has the appearance of good" (*ST* II-II, 49, 8, respondeo). Or, to put it in more Ignatian terms, when tempting good people, evil spirits are more inclined to disguise themselves as angels of light in order to distract those good souls from the greater good and thus lead them astray.

In order to overcome such insidious temptations, we need to exercise prudence, that is, to apply right reason to action. For, without prudence we risk either choosing poorly or choosing not at all. But even opting not to make a decision is to make a decision and generally to make a poor one at that. By not discerning priorities among the many goods to be done and thus failing to embrace the greater good, we end up like Martha—distracted by too much serving. That distraction ultimately impedes any good that we could have hoped to have accomplished. It is no wonder that decision-making can paralyze an individual. Martha was "anxious and troubled about many things" because she had failed to discern the greater good, the one thing necessary, the good portion which her sister Mary quietly enjoyed. Mary's freedom from anxiety was in itself a great gift which the Lord had given to her. In order to strengthen the virtue of prudence which Mary possessed naturally, the good Lord gave her the supernatural gift of counsel (cf. *ST* II-II, 52. 1-4). By this gift of the Holy Spirit, explains Saint Thomas, "God moves the mind of the wayfarer in matters of action, by soothing the pre-existing anxiety of doubt" (*ST* II-II, 52, 3, respondeo). Thus did God's grace inspire Mary as indeed it aids all the faithful to discern properly, to avoid Satan's snares, to identify the greater good and to embrace it in freedom. Or, to put it in more colloquial terms, the gift of counsel enables us to keep calm and carry on. By God's gracious gift we are freed from anxious distractions in order to receive His further gifts. Thus not only did Mary, along with her saintly sister Martha, receive Jesus into her home, but seated tranquilly at His feet she also received what He Himself had to offer.

The Gospel account of Martha and Mary speaks powerfully to priests engaged in the active life of pastoral ministry. While longing for the contemplative tranquility, which Mary enjoyed, we priests can all too easily be overcome by the anxious distractions, which plagued Martha. The many demands of the contemporary apostolate threaten to overwhelm us. Like Martha we often find ourselves distracted with much serving, anxious and troubled about many things. This is particularly true of the diocesan clergy. As the number of priests has decreased in recent decades, parish clusters have been formed in order to assure a priestly presence in every parochial community. The danger is that one priest can still only do the daily work of one priest even if he must now cover three or four parish churches placed under his sole jurisdiction. More and more priests find themselves spread thinner and thinner with workloads becoming heavier and heavier. Great burdens are often prematurely placed upon the shoulders of younger priests not only because they are deemed to have more energy, but also because, given the priest shortage, there seems to be no alternative. Yet are these younger priests ready to assume such weighty responsibilities before they themselves have had the necessary time to mature in their own priesthood? The risks are significant whether one be newly ordained or a veteran member of the clergy. For, a priest can keep up with such excessive apostolic demands only for so long before he himself becomes the next crisis, that is, before his own physical, psychological and spiritual health collapses.

For the sake of the Gospel, the good of the Church, the salvation of souls and the wellbeing of the priest himself, priests must be encouraged to serve prudently and magnanimously. In this regard, priests ranked among the Church's saints rightly serve as our models. For, these men were heroically virtuous, which means among other things that they were *heroically prudent*. In an exemplary manner, those saintly priests prudently discerned the greater good among the many goods to be done, they set aside the lesser goods, entrusting them to others, and they wholeheartedly dedicated themselves to the greater service which they had discerned. Such heroically prudent priests were truly magnanimous men. They did not succumb to the temptation of micromanagement. They were "not over-anxious about many things, but [were] confident and unworried over matters where [they] ought to have trust" (*ST* II-II, 47, 9, reply 3). They sought the *magis*—the more which the less contains. They knew how to make sacrifices for the greater good and to channel their forces accordingly. Their prudent way of proceeding finds eloquent expression in the wise words once spoken by a north German Bishop to his young priest-secretary: "I will not always be able to do what is beautiful nor even what is necessary; I simply can do what I can do." The good Bishop practiced magnanimity. He faithfully dedicated himself to the less which was more.

The prophet Elijah's encounter with the Lord on Mount Horeb illustrates well the challenges of the contemporary apostolate and the need for proper discernment in the midst of them:

> Behold, the Lord passed by, and a great and strong wind rent the mountains, and broke in pieces the rocks before the Lord, but the Lord was not in the wind; and after the wind an earthquake, but the Lord was not in the earthquake; and after the earthquake a fire, but the Lord was not in the fire; and after the fire a still small voice. And when Elijah heard it, he wrapped his face in his mantle and went out and stood at the entrance of the cave (1 Kings 19:11-13).

The scene is one of sensory overload. The strong wind, earthquake and fire threaten to mute the Lord's still small voice or at least to deafen Elijah to His call. How often do the wind, earthquake and fire of our apostolic lives threaten to disorient us in our priestly ministry! Distracted by much serving we priests struggle to behold the Lord and to hear His voice. Too much serving ironically distracts us like Martha from the One whom we serve. The technology, which was meant to facilitate our work, only complicates the situation. We are bombarded by emails, text messages, Facebook updates, images and information galore. We suffer from an information overload, and in the midst of all these distractions we can fail to discern the presence of the Lord and listen to His voice. If this information overload is coupled with even the slightest messianic complex on the priest's part, the priest finds himself driven to do more and more. With Saint Paul he strives to be all things for all men, which in itself is not a bad thing. But once the Evil One has manipulated this otherwise good desire, the priest pushes himself to the point of exhaustion, aiming at an availability which is not only not humanly possible, but would also tax beyond its limits the mystical gift of bilocation! Such a priest eventually notes that his exhaustive labors produce increasingly diminished returns. If he does not prudently pull back, he will collapse, and the Evil One will have succeeded in undermining his ministry. Such imprudent service will leave him unable to help anyone, even himself. The remedy for this grave ill is the magnanimity which enabled Elijah to perceive the Lord's quiet presence in the midst of the raging storm.

The magnanimous priest follows Elijah's example. Firstly, he stands truly indifferent before all created goods and thus enjoys the necessary freedom to discern the greater good. Secondly, the magnanimous priest knows how to make life-giving sacrifices, to set aside lesser goods, entrusting them to others, so that he can dedicate himself to the greater good of his priestly ministry—most especially, to the worship of God. Thirdly, in order to make such sacrifices, he has learned how to say 'no' skillfully, which is by no means an easy task for a generous soul dedicated to the service of others, but nonetheless a necessary task if he is going to be able to persevere in his service in a fruitful and healthy manner. The magnanimous priest takes to heart the Lord's command: "Let what you say be simply 'Yes' or 'No'; anything more than this comes from evil" (Matthew 5:37). Thus, in obedience to the Lord, he has learned to say 'no' even to good, beautiful and necessary things in order to be able to say 'yes' to the greater good of his priestly ministry. Fourthly, he develops good habits. He grows in virtue. He follows a personal rule of life which orders his day, allowing, nonetheless, for the flexibility needed to respond to legitimate demands as they arise. Prayer is foundational for his rule of life. In order to serve with Martha freed from anxiety, he sits daily with Mary at the feet of Jesus. He meets the Lord each and every day in the Eucharist. He prays daily, and he faithfully observes the Sabbath, that is, he takes his day-off each week in order to rest in body, mind and spirit. His annual retreat provides him with the singular grace of dedicating himself exclusively to the greatest good of his priestly life and ministry: the worship of God which restores his soul and

JOSEPH CAROLA, SJ

revives his drooping spirits. Regular confession reorients his
soul when sin threatens to lead him astray. Sleep and recreation also form an important part of his rule of life. For, if
we neglect the legitimate needs of mind and body, we risk
jeopardizing the good of our souls—we are, after all, incarnate beings. Finally, the magnanimous priest follows Saint
Ignatius' sage advice: *age quod agis*. He is about what he is
about. He resists the temptation to multitask. He is not taken
simultaneously here and there by much serving. Rather, in
having identified the greater good of the present moment,
he dedicates himself wholly to it. Consequently, his manner
is leisurely and slow. As Aristotle and Saint Thomas note,
having the aptitude for magnanimity, the magnanimous person demonstrates a natural disposition for its accidents.[14] His
voice is not shrill, his speech not rushed and his step not
hurried. Rather, he radiates a certain *gravitas*, which is not
off-putting, but, on the contrary, reassuring.

At the miraculous resurrection of her brother Lazarus,
Martha, no longer anxious and troubled about many things,
revealed the true depths of her sanctity. Upon hearing that
the Lord Jesus was approaching Bethany, she went out to
meet Him. This time, however, it was she who rebuked Him:
"Lord, if you had been here, my brother would not have
died" (John 11:21). Yet even then she trusted that God
would grant whatever He asked. In the midst of her sorrow,

---

[14] Cf. ARISTOTLE, *Nichomachean Ethics* 1125ª14-17; THOMAS AQUINAS, *In
Decem Libros Ethicorum Aristotelis ad Nicomachum Expositio* § 782.

Martha kept her gazed fixed solely upon the Lord and professed her faith in Him. "Yes, Lord," she declared, "I believe that you are the Christ, the Son of God, he who is coming into the world" (John 11:27). Like the prophet Elijah, she had learned to hear His voice despite threatening distractions. Like her sister Mary, she devoutly sought the one thing necessary, life in Christ Jesus, and it was not to be taken from her. On account of her faith, moreover, life was restored to her brother Lazarus as well. Thus we learn from Saint Martha that serving the Lord magnanimously gives life to both the one who serves and those whom he serves. Anything to the contrary comes from the Evil One and should be prudently ignored.

Baltimore, 28 July 2014
Iowa City, 8 August 2014

VII

A BLESSED BREAKING
ON VERDANT PASTURES
Serving the Lord faithfully in our poverty

Gospel: John 6:1-15

From among His disciples Jesus called twelve to whom
he gave "power and authority over all demons and to cure
diseases" (Luke 9:1). These men He sent out "to preach the
kingdom of God and to heal" (Luke 9:2). Going from village
to village they preached in poverty the Good News of our
salvation. They drove out demons and cured the sick. Tired
from their apostolic labors, they returned to Jesus "and told
him all that they had done and taught" (Mark 6:31). Recognizing their meritorious exhaustion, Jesus invited them to retreat "to a lonely place, and rest a while. For many were
coming and going, and they had no leisure even to eat"
(Mark 6:31). So, they withdrew by themselves and went by
boat across the Sea of Galilee to a lonely place. But even
then they could not escape the constant demands of the
apostolate into which they had only recently been inducted.
For, the crowds, having discovered their destination, quickly

followed them by foot and arrived at Tabgha ahead of them. The crowds eagerly pursued Jesus and His Apostles because they had witnessed the many signs which Jesus had performed. They had heard the Twelve preach, and by their ministry they had been healed in body, mind and spirit. Through the Gospel they had found solace in their misery, and they would not be separated from its healing balm. Consequently, in droves, they flocked to Jesus and the Twelve, leaving them not even a moment's rest.

As Jesus and the Apostles approached the shore, they beheld a multitude of people. What had been a lonely place at the foot of the Mount of Beatitudes had become another field of mission. Christ and the Twelve had withdrawn from the crowds in order to seek rest from their apostolic labors, but the demands of charity followed them. At the sight of the great throng, Jesus' Heart was moved with pity "and he had compassion on them, because they were like sheep without a shepherd" (Mark 6:34). Always the Good Shepherd, Christ "welcomed them and spoke to them of the kingdom of God, and cured those who had need of healing" (Luke 9:11). As evening drew near the already exhausted Apostles implored Jesus to send the crowds away so that they could buy food for themselves in the neighboring villages. But to their amazement Jesus insisted that the Apostles themselves give them something to eat. His instruction left the Twelve dumbfounded. They were poor, exhausted men. How could they ever manage to amass sufficient provisions in order to feed over five-thousand men, women and children?

While the Synoptic Gospels only tersely relate Jesus' exchange with His disciples, the Fourth Gospel recounts their dialogue in greater detail. Saint John the Evangelist notes that it was Jesus Himself who initiated the conversation and, by means of an effectively rhetorical question, He purposefully provoked the Apostles' rather desperate response. Jesus asked Philip: "How are we to buy bread, so that these people may eat?" (John 6:5). Jesus questioned Philip simply to test him, John explains, "for he himself knew what he would do" (John 6:6). The ever practical Philip responded that two-hundred denarii—basically an entire year's wages—would not suffice to purchase enough bread to satisfy so large a crowd. For his part Andrew, Simon Peter's brother, found among the people a lad with five barley loaves and two fish, but he rightly asked: "What are they among so many?" (John 6:9). Poor and exhausted from their labors, the Apostles appraised the situation and sought concrete—even though admittedly futile—solutions to the quickly developing food crisis. In the end they could do little more than admit their poverty, their notable lack of resources and their utter insufficiency in responding to such overwhelming apostolic demands. Can we really fault them for imploring the Lord to send the crowds away?

The demands of our contemporary apostolic mission are often similarly overwhelming. Priests working in parishes, schools, diocesan chancelleries, various chaplaincies and almost every other apostolate are pulled in multiple directions. The pastoral needs of God's people are great and only grow greater. The harvest is indeed plenty, but the laborers remain few. While technology has increased our availability for ministry, it has also assured that there is no escaping the crowds even when we retreat to a lonely place. By making us constantly available, our smartphones have effectively out-smarted us! But unlike the technological instruments which we employ in the contemporary apostolate, we ourselves are not machines. We need regular rest if we hope to persevere in our apostolic labors. In seeking such rest we acknowledge honestly and humbly our own apostolic limitations. We may be very talented men with a great capacity for work. But no matter how great our talents, they, too, have their limits. The service of the Gospel, which employs our talents for God's greater glory, will always transcend the outer limits of our natural abilities. Given the immense and ever increasing de-mands of the contemporary apostolate, even a talented and highly capable priest cannot avoid having to confront his own personal limitations. Like the Apostles at Tabgha, we priests stand in our poverty before the multitude, whom we serve, and with a certain trepidation we ask ourselves how the thousands are to be fed with only the five loaves and two fish which we possess.

As we have noted, Saint John tells us that, even before interrogating Philip, Jesus already knew what He Himself would do. But He first had to lead the Apostles to an au-thentic recognition of their own personal poverty in order to uproot all pride from their hearts and minds. Generous men typically answer the call to serve in the Lord's vineyard. They zealously sacrifice themselves for the sake of the Gospel in loving imitation of Christ Crucified. An appar-ently limitless generosity often characterizes the lives of the newly ordained. Their zeal is indeed laudable. But every priest—both young and old—must purge his zeal of all pos-sibly Pelagian tendencies. He should recall that the widow who gave her all did so not from her strength and surplus, but from her poverty (cf. Luke 21:1-4). With profound humility the priest must recognize that he is nothing more than an earthen vessel containing a most precious treasure in order "to show that the transcendent power [of his priestly ministry] belongs to God and not to [himself]" (2 Corinthians 4:7b). The prudent priest, who frankly appraises his own limitations, knows full and well that without Jesus he can do nothing. In the psalmist's words he humbly acknowledges that, "unless the Lord builds the house, those who build it labor in vain" (Psalm 127:1). The multitude will indeed be fed—not, however, by means of the priest's own unaided zealous efforts, but rather by Christ's grace enriching his poverty. Christ's "power [will be] made perfect in [his] weakness" (2 Corinthians 12:9). On this account, along with Saint Paul, the priest rightly insists: "I will all the more gladly boast of my weakness, that the power of Christ may rest upon me" (2 Corinthians 12:9). Confident in Christ he serenely embraces his poverty in order to serve the Lord in holiness and humility.

Before miraculously multiplying the loaves and the fish, Jesus commanded the crowds to sit down. "Now there was much grass in that place," Saint John relates (John 6:10). Saint Mark emphasizes that the grass was green (cf. Mark 6:39). This reference to green grass is not insignificant, for it harkens back to the twenty-third psalm: "The Lord is my shepherd, I shall not want; he makes me lie down in green pastures. He leads me beside still waters; he restores my soul" (Psalm 23:1-3a). Although initially provoking no little anxiety in the Apostles, this evangelical scene is, in fact, one of refreshment, tranquility and peace. For, it is Christ the Good Shepherd Himself who, by blessing and breaking the Apostles' poverty, both dispels their fears and feeds the multitude. With clear Eucharistic overtones, Saint Matthew recounts that blessed breaking on those verdant pastures: "[T]aking the five loaves and the two fish [Jesus] looked up to heaven, and blessed, and broke and gave the loaves to the disciples, and the disciples gave them to the crowds" (Matthew 14:19). Only in that blessed breaking did that miraculous multiplication occur. Taking place at Passover that blessed breaking prefigured the blessed breaking of the Good Shepherd Himself who at the Last Supper and on Calvary Hill would lay down His life for His sheep.

We priests, who minister *in persona Christi capitis*, recognize ourselves not only in that young lad who offers the Lord his meager fare, but also in that bread blessed and broken. Through the Sacrament of Holy Orders, we have been conformed to Christ Crucified whose Body and Blood we offer under the accidents of bread and wine as a Holy Sacrifice truly pleasing to God the Father. Like Christ the Bread of Life, we, too, are a bread broken so that others may be fed and live. In imitation of Christ, we priests are called to pour ourselves out in His service by loving our neighbor as Christ has loved us unto death on the cross. Just as Christ's death has restored our life, our priestly outpouring is to be likewise life-giving for both ourselves and those whom we serve. Consequently, it is not a matter of imprudently breaking ourselves in a frenzied apostolic service which suffocates our prayer. Such a breaking would be fruitless, crippling and ultimately destructive. No, it is rather a *blessed* breaking—a vivifying outpouring made possible only through Christ's grace prayerfully received. Christ the Good Shepherd blesses and breaks us not to destroy us, but rather to produce abundant life in us and through us in those whom we serve. Of this blessed breaking Saint Paul writes most eloquently: "We are afflicted in every way, but not crushed; perplexed, but not driven to despair; persecuted, but not forsaken; struck down, but not destroyed; always carrying in the body the death of Jesus, so that the life of Jesus may also be manifested in our bodies" (2 Corinthians 4: 8-10). Just as Cleopas and his companion at Emmaus came to know Jesus in the breaking of the bread, so too those whom we selflessly serve come to see in us through our blessed breaking the Risen Lord Jesus Crucified. For, having been blessed and broken—in other words, having been crucified with Christ—"it is no longer [we] who live, but Christ who lives in [us]" (Galatians 2:20).

In this blessed breaking, which our priesthood entails, we are indeed broken and given to others. We are poured out and emptied in Christ's service, and yet mysteriously, paradoxically and indeed miraculously by means of this blessed breaking our capacity to love increases. Saint John recounts that "when [the crowds] had eaten their fill, [Jesus] told his disciples, 'Gather up the fragments left over, that nothing may be lost.' So they gathered them up and filled twelve baskets with fragments from the five barley loaves, left by those who had eaten" (John 6:12-13). Those twelve baskets filled with fragments symbolize the hundredfold of love and grace promised to those who abandon all in order to follow Jesus. The priest, who through Christ's grace gives of himself completely in love, ultimately receives more from the Lord than his own poverty could have ever produced. For, the good Lord cannot be outdone in generosity. Yes, we are broken in His service, but Christ Himself consolingly reassures us that none of the abundant fragments which remain—not even the slightest morsel—will be lost.

Instructing that the fragments be carefully gathered, the Lord imparts wisdom—the wisdom to discern properly between the movements of the good and the evil spirit. The Evil One would have us think fallaciously that the blessed breaking of our priestly life and ministry entails the abandonment of whatever fragments remain—in other words, that it entails self-neglect. He would subtly infiltrate our good desires for selfless service and have us neglect the legitimate demands of caring for our own physical, mental and spiritual wellbeing. But remember that we are to love our neighbor as we love ourselves. Failure to care for our own health undermines our loving care of neighbor. For, the poor health, which results from such neglect, threatens to deny the Lord the years of priestly ministry to which He calls us. He may call us to serve Him in sickness rather than health. If so, He will give us the grace to embrace our illness with serenity, and our illness itself will become the blessed instrument of His grace in our lives and the lives of others. But we should not succumb to the wicked designs of the Evil One, who harasses us with anxieties, and make ourselves ill through neglect. Such negligence has nothing to do with selfless service, and it is opposed to God's will. For, while it is indeed a breaking, it is not the blessed breaking of the Lord.

As we experience the Lord's blessed breaking, let us recall that the Apostles did not endure it alone. At Tabgha, when the Lord commissioned them to provide in their poverty for the hungry multitude, an apostolic brotherhood bound the Twelve together. Together they labored in distributing that blessed, broken bread to the crowds reclining on those green fields. When we priests are blessed and broken in the Lord's service, we, too, are never alone. Our priesthood unites us, and our priestly fraternity sustains us. Priestly friendships especially help to relieve the stress which can easily mount as apostolic demands threaten to overwhelm us. Saint Paul himself benefitted from such relief. "Our bodies had no rest," the Apostle writes of himself, "but we were afflicted at every turn—fighting without and fear within. But God, who comforts the downcast, comforted us by the coming of Titus" (2 Corinthians 7:5-6). Paul found much needed relief in Titus's companionship. Imitating Saint Paul may we never hesitate to turn to our brothers in times of need. May we also be good brothers to our fellow priests when they are downcast and experience more acutely the stress of our priestly life and ministry. For, such priestly fraternity is an essential part of the Lord's blessing which renders fruitful our being broken in His service.

Finally, Saint John tells us that the crowds, having recognized Jesus as the prophet who was to come into the world, sought to take Him by force and to make Him king. But "Jesus withdrew again to the mountain by himself" (John 6:15). The day would eventually come when Jesus would allow the crowds to take Him by force and make Him king, crowning Him with thorns and nailing Him to the cross. But at present, in their misguided enthusiasm, they wanted to make Him an earthly king, and Christ eluded them. There is a final lesson here for us priests to learn. We are not to build an earthly kingdom for ourselves in the parishes, schools, chancelleries, chaplaincies or any other apostolate where we may minister to the People of God. The priest, who fails to acknowledge his own poverty, can all too easily succumb to this temptation. He zealously labors to build his own house, but he does so without Christ. Even though he may meet with a certain success and acclaim, he ultimately labors in vain. For, he feeds his own ego rather than Christ's flock. In contrast, Christ paradoxically feeds the multitude not through the priest's personal strength, but rather through his poverty. It is the priest's humble, holy witness—not his material success—which inspires in the faithful a true love of the Lord. May we never forget that we serve a Crucified Lord and that as Christians we measure success by the standard of His Cross. To counteract any misguided illusions of messianic grandeur, may we conclude each day, prayerfully protesting before the Lord: "We are unworthy servants; we have only done what was our duty" (Luke 17:10).

My brothers, one day as Christ's priests, each of you must take up his own cross daily and follow after Jesus. Your cross will entail real suffering, but do not fear it. Rather recognize in it the blessed breaking of Tabgha. Yes, you will be broken in the Lord's service. At certain moments you will experience that breaking more acutely than at other times. When this occurs, keep your eyes fixed firmly upon the Lord's right hand raised in blessing. Know that His grace sustains you and enriches your poverty so that the multitude, whom you serve, may be fed. As you experience being broken, live in the grace of His blessing. You will live in that blessing through personal prayer, meditation upon the Scriptures and the Eucharist. Your prayer will lead you into an intimate union with Christ Jesus. He will draw you into the depths of His pierced Heart and bathe you in His mercy. Such profound communion with Our Lord is the blessing which will sustain you in that sacerdotal breaking. Be confident that the Christ, who blesses and breaks, also gathers up the fragments so that nothing may be lost. Hear Him exclaim: "Come to me all who labor and are heavy laden, and I will give you rest" (Matthew 11:28). As you prayerfully approach Him, He will have you lie down upon the green grass where He Himself will feed you and revive your drooping spirits.

Baltimore, 30 July 2014
Iowa City, 9 August 2014

VIII

THE PRIESTHOOD AND THE CROSS
Bearing the other's burden in imitation of Christ Crucified

First Reading: Colossians 1:15 - 20
Gospel: Luke 5:33 – 39

During the rite of priestly ordination before the imposition of hands, the bishop questions the deacon about his
intentions. In this solemn dialogue the deacon makes his sacerdotal promises. Concluding this sacred interrogation, the
bishop asks: "Are you resolved to consecrate your life to God
for the salvation of his people, and to unite yourself more
closely every day to Christ the High Priest, who offered himself for us to the Father as a perfect sacrifice?" The deacon
responds: "I am, with the help of God." The deacon publicly
professes his deep desire to unite himself more closely every
day to Christ the High Priest, to be united with Christ the
Pure Victim and to offer himself as Christ did to the Father
for the salvation of all men and women.

Let us carefully consider the exact implications of this
sacred exchange between the bishop and the deacon. The
deacon is not simply asked if he wishes to be united to Christ

the High Priest. The question is not an invitation to a subtle form of clericalism. For Christ is not only priest, but He is also victim. Upon the Cross Christ the High Priest offers Himself as a pure victim to the Father for us and for our salvation. Therefore, the priestly union with Christ, which the deacon desires, is essentially a self-immolation with Christ. The deacon solemnly expresses his desire to consecrate himself to God together with Christ Crucified—that is, to sacrifice himself together with Christ upon the Cross for the salvation of all men and women. The deacon also realizes that, while his sacerdotal self-offering begins with his priestly ordination, it will come to completion only as he breathes his last breath. He promises that he is resolved to unite himself more closely every day to Christ the High Priest and Pure Victim. He desires to be conformed ever more closely to Christ Crucified, to share ever more intimately in Christ's Cross which the Lord bore for the salvation of all men and women. To make such a promise is humanly impossible. On this account, the deacon humbly answers the bishop: "I am, with the help of God"—because without the help of God, without His grace, to carry such a cross would overwhelm and ultimately destroy the man. But with the grace of the Crucified and Risen Lord to whom he is more closely united every day, the newly ordained bears his own sacerdotal cross in a manner salvific not only for himself, but also for those whom he serves.

Later, during the same rite of ordination, after the anointing of the newly ordained priest's hands, the bishop presents him with the gifts of bread and wine, saying: "Accept from the holy people of God the gifts to be offered to him.

Know what you are doing, and imitate the mystery you celebrate: model your life on the mystery of the Lord's cross."
Thus is the newly ordained priest immediately reminded of
the promise which he has just made—the solemn promise to
conform his life to the mystery of the Cross of Christ the
High Priest and Pure Victim. Here the promise is framed
within an explicitly Eucharistic context—the moment of the
offering of the gifts by the people. Let us consider the sacramental depths of the priest's encounter with God's holy people as they offer the gifts for the Eucharistic sacrifice.

When the people offer their gifts for sacrifice, whom
do they encounter in the priest? When the priest receives
their offering, whom does he meet in those who make this
sacred offering? In the priest the people meet Christ the
High Priest and Pure Victim to whom the priest is sacramentally united. They meet the *alter Christus caput*. In the people
the priest encounters the members of Christ's Body in
whom abides the image of the living God, in whom with the
eyes of faith one discerns the Face of Christ—often the
Face of the Suffering Christ. What do the holy people offer
for the Eucharistic sacrifice? Bread and wine. Yes, bread and
wine. But this bread and wine symbolize the totality of their
own lives which they themselves offer in order to be consecrated to God. As he enters into his newly ordained ministry,
the young priest quickly recognizes that in this Eucharistic
offering he symbolically receives the other's daily sacrifices
in order to unite them with the unique Sacrifice of Christ by
means of which the Father reconciles to Himself all things,
making peace through the Blood of His Cross (cf. Colossians 1:20).

When they encounter their priest, whether it take place in church or on the street, in the confessional or in their ordinary daily exchanges, God's people trustingly unburden themselves of all that weighs down heavily upon them. They share with him their sufferings and confess to him their sins as they seek the good Lord's consolation and mercy. It is not the priest's own personal merits but rather Christ's grace which inspires their confidence in him. In imitation of Christ, the priest receives their offering—that is, he takes upon himself their burdens and sufferings as Christ Crucified took upon Himself our sins. Thus, in the very act of receiving the holy people's oblation, the priest is ever more closely united to the Crucified Christ, High Priest and Pure Victim. In receiving the other's burden, the priest works for the other's salvation, alleviating the other's often profound pain as he listens compassionately during their encounter. Through the ministry of His priest, whether it be at the Altar where he offers the Eucharistic bread and wine or in the confessional where he imparts divine mercy, Christ comforts the other and heals him. Thus, the bishop rightly admonishes the newly ordained priest: "Know what you are doing, and imitate the mystery you celebrate: model your life on the mystery of the Lord's cross."

Let us return now to the words "more closely every day" which form part of the initial exchange between the bishop and the man to be ordained priest. These words indicate a continual growth in the life of the priest—an ever more profound sharing in the Lord's Cross. It is true that at his ordination the priest is completely conformed in the depths of his being to Christ the High Priest and Pure Victim. He lacks nothing sacramentally as he ministers *in persona Christi capitis*—in the person of Christ the Head. But in terms of his own personal apprehension of what his ordination has entailed, he should strive daily to delve more deeply into the mystery of his newly ordained life. He needs time to grow in his priestly life and to mature in his priestly ministry. In this sense the newly ordained priest resembles the new wine of today's Gospel which one does not put into old wineskins without danger. The hide of new wineskins made precisely for new wine is taut, and it expands only gradually as the wine ages. Similarly, I would say, one ought not to stretch the newly ordained priest beyond his own limits. It does the young priest a disservice when he is immediately given great pastoral responsibilities—that is, when new wine is put into old wineskins. New wine should be put into new wineskins. One should carefully look after the vocation of the newly ordained priest so that the cross which he bears from the start does not paralyze him. For this reason the bishop usually entrusts the newly ordained to the guidance of a wise pastor with ample experience. But I would say that the holy people of God should also realize their own particular and no less necessary role in taking care of the newly ordained priest who has consecrated himself to God in Christ for their salvation.

Love your priests—especially the youngest. Help them to live their priestly vocation faithfully. Help them to bear their cross with Christ so that they may mature in their ministry of taking upon themselves your sufferings, your burdens and your sins—along with their own—and uniting these offerings to the unique Sacrifice of Christ in the Holy

Eucharist. Thus, with the help of God and the fraternal support of the ecclesial community, the new wine of the newly ordained priest may become the old wine which is declared good—good because it has matured in the crucible of suffering. It matures through the newly ordained priest's own suffering and the sufferings of the holy people which he faithfully receives and offers to the Lord. In fact, this new wine will mature only through the Cross of the Crucified Christ to whom the priest is more closely united every day for sake of the salvation of God's holy people.

Cagliari, 6 September 2013

IX

A FIRST MASS OF THANKSGIVING, BRAINERD, MINNESOTA
Ministering Word and Sacrament both in and out of season

First Reading: 2 Chronicles 24:17-25
Gospel: Matthew 6:24-34

Yesterday on the liturgical memorial of the sixteenth-century English martyrs, Saints Thomas More and John Fisher, at the beginning of the *Fortnight for Freedom* promoted by the United States Conference of Catholic Bishops, in Duluth's Cathedral Church of Our Lady of the Rosary, Seth Gogolin was ordained a priest of Jesus Christ. Father Gogolin was ordained to preach God's Word and to administer His holy Sacraments. Today's readings from the *Second Book of Chronicles* and the *Gospel of Saint Matthew* providentially address this twofold ministry of Word and Sacrament which is now his. The first reading calls Father Gogolin to proclaim God's Word with steadfast courage. The Gospel, read in the light of today's celebration, reveals the sacramental graces which Father Gogolin has himself received and is called to minister to others.

The *Second Book of Chronicles* recounts how the Hebrew people following King Joash and the princes of Judah had abandoned the God of their fathers. It also narrates the courageous witness unto death of the priestly prophet Zechariah who spoke out against their betrayal. Joash had become King of Judah at the very young age of seven, and he reigned for forty years. Throughout much of his reign, the King received wise counsel from Zechariah's father, the priest Jehoiada. "And Joash," Scripture tells us, "did what was right in the eyes of the Lord all the days of Jehoiada the priest" (2 Chronicles 24:2). The King restored the Lord's Temple in Jerusalem which had fallen into disrepair. Together with Jehoiada he provided worthy vessels for divine worship. But after the priest's death, the princely leaders of the people gathered about the King and convinced him to abandon the right worship God for pagan idolatry. Sadly, the Hebrew people allowed their leaders to lead them astray. Thus as a nation they forsook their religious heritage. The Lord, calling them back to Himself, sent prophets among them to admonish them. But they obstinately ignored their prophetic warnings. Finally, the deceased priest Jehoiada's own son, inspired by God's Spirit, spoke out boldly. Zechariah preached God's Word, emphasizing the dire consequences of their act, "[b]ut they conspired against him, and by command of the king they stoned him with stones in the court of the house of the Lord" (2 Chronicles 24:21). By way of prefigurement "the blood of Zechariah, who perished between the altar and the sanctuary" (Luke 11:51), speaks eloquently of the Catholic priest's ordained mission to preach God's Word not only in season, but indeed even more importantly out of season.

Father Gogolin has been ordained to proclaim Christ's saving Gospel without compromise, to wield the two-edged sword of Sacred Scripture which like the surgeon's scalpel cuts deeply in order to heal. He has been ordained to speak the Truth which saves, to speak it at once humbly and yet fearlessly. As Saint Paul once exhorted the young Saint Timothy, the Apostle likewise exhorts the newly ordained: "Preach the word, be urgent in season and out of season, convince, rebuke, and exhort, be unfailing in patience and in teaching. For the time is coming when people will not endure sound teaching, but having itching ears they will accumulate for themselves teachers to suit their own likings and will turn away from listening to the truth and wander into myths" (2 Timothy 4:2-4). Paul prepares both Timothy and the contemporary preacher of the Word for a mission similar to Zechariah's, commanding further: "always be steady, endure suffering, do the work of an evangelist, fulfill your ministry" (2 Timothy 4:5).

Father Gogolin, hear Saint Paul urgently address these words to you today. For, we live in an age which rejects sound teaching. Many readily set aside the Truth of Christ for a merely apparent good. A rampant relativism renders faith and morals meaningless. Marriage and the family are arbitrarily redefined. Religious liberty throughout the world and indeed even in our own nation is under threat. In the United States of America, there are those who would drastically reduce religious liberty to a freedom of worship restricted to our homes and church buildings in a deliberate attempt to remove Christ's Gospel from the public square. Father Gogolin, in this historical moment you have been ordained to preach the saving Truth of Christ's Gospel both in season and out of season. "The courage and zeal for this task cannot be obtained from another," the American Successors of the Apostles remind us priests during this *Fortnight for Freedom*, "it must be rooted in your own concern for your flock and nourished by the graces you received at your ordination" (USCCB, *Our First, Most Cherished Liberty: A Statement on Religious Liberty*, 2012)—graces which you received only yesterday on the feast day of the English martyrs Thomas More and John Fisher who, like Zechariah, having witnessed to the truth, were killed at a king's command.

An attentive reading of today's Gospel within the liturgical context of this First Mass of Thanksgiving brings to light the graces of yesterday's ordination. Preaching atop a hill overlooking the Sea of Galilee, Jesus exhorts His disciples not to be anxious about food, drink or clothing. He assures them and indeed us all that our heavenly Father will provide for us in ways far exceeding our expectations. Indeed, yesterday, our heavenly Father clothed Seth Gogolin with the grace of the priesthood so that through Seth's priesthood He may nourish us with the Body and Blood of Jesus His Son.

Let us consider this evangelical passage more closely. Firstly, we should note that a father clothing his son is not an indifferent act in Scripture. Jacob clothed the son of his old age, Joseph, in a long robe with sleeves for he loved him more than any of his other children (cf. Genesis 37:3). When the prodigal son's compassionate father welcomed his repentant son home, he quickly clothed him with the best robe that he possessed (cf. Luke 15:22). Not simply with mere garments did these fathers clothe their sons. They clothed them above all else in mercy and love. The psalmist tells us explicitly that God clothes His priests in holiness (cf. Psalm 132:9). In His merciful love for both Seth and all those whom Seth will serve, God has clothed him in holiness, that is, with the sacerdotal grace of Holy Orders. In the very depths of his being, Seth has been conformed to Christ the High Priest—to Christ the Head of His ecclesial Body the Church for whom Christ offers Himself upon the Cross. Seth can now say with Saint Paul in a way as never before: "I have been crucified with Christ; it is no longer I who live, but Christ who lives in me" (Galatians 2:20). The priestly stole and chasuble, with which he was clothed yesterday and now wears, majestically symbolize this new and irrevocable reality.

In virtue of these Holy Orders, Seth will speak the very 'I' of Jesus when offering the Eucharist and absolving sins. Standing at the altar and seated in the confessional, he will proclaim: "This is *My* Body, this is the Chalice of *My* Blood; *I* absolve you from your sins." Only the man whom the Father has clothed with the sacerdotal grace of His Son's Headship can utter these saving words which effect what they signify. Soon he will speak the words of consecration for the sake of our salvation, offering Christ's unique Sacrifice to the Father, transforming ordinary bread and wine into the Body and Blood of His Son. From the altar, with anointed hands, he will minister to us the Bread of Life and the Chalice of Eternal Salvation. Elsewhere, in the confessional, as he raises his hand in absolution, Christ will remit the contritely confessed sins of those for whom He has shed His Blood. On this account, the psalmists tells us further that God's faithful people rejoice (cf. Psalm 132:9). For, we need no longer worry about food, drink or clothing. We rejoice rather because our heavenly Father has sacramentally clothed His son Seth with the priesthood of Christ His Eternal Son made man in order to nourish us with the Eucharist and to absolve us from our sins.

Father Gogolin, one final word. While it is true that the validity of the Sacraments, which you will celebrate, in no way depend upon your personal holiness, your personal holiness is, nonetheless, by no means irrelevant to your priestly life and ministry. Your grace-inspired pursuit of holiness will directly enhance the credibility of the Word, which you preach, and the Sacraments, which you administer. On this account, Jesus exhorts you to seek first the Kingdom of God and His righteousness before you can credibly preach and minister His life-giving Word and Sacraments to others. May you yourself be the first to be converted by the Word which you preach. May you yourself first come to know Christ's mercy when contritely confessing your own sins in order to speak convincingly of Christ's mercy to others. May you yourself daily eat Christ's Body and drink His Blood so that you will have the spiritual strength to be God's ordained instrument in feeding others. May you seek first God's Kingdom and His holiness not simply for the sake of your own salvation, but also for the sake of those whom you serve. For, you will serve them best not by means of your innumerable pastoral duties, but rather by being a holy priest in whom they clearly behold the Merciful Face of Christ.

Brainerd, 23 June 2012
Saturday of the Eleventh Week in Ordinary Time

X

A MASS OF THANKSGIVING, ROME
Faithfully celebrating the sacred mysteries

First Reading: 1 Chronicles 15:3-4, 15-16; 16:1-2
Gospel: Luke 1:39-47

When the Diocesan Bishop of Joliet in Illinois exam-
ined the then-Deacon Michael Pawlowicz at his sacerdotal
ordination one week ago today, he inquired: "Are you resolved to celebrate the mysteries of Christ faithfully and re-
ligiously as the Church has handed them down to us for the
glory of God and the sanctification of Christ's people?" According to the prescribed ritual Michael dutifully responded:
"I am." Even though not present in the Joliet Cathedral last
Saturday morning, Michael's Roman friends can easily imag-
ine the deep devotion with which he would have responded
to that particular question. Among the triple *munera* of the
priestly office is the *munus sanctificandi*—the charge of sanc-
tifying God's people particularly through the administration
of the Sacraments. To that end, after the imposition of
hands and the recitation of the consecratory prayer, the
Bishop anointed Michael's hands, saying, "The Father

anointed our Lord Jesus Christ through the power of the Holy Spirit. May Jesus preserve you to sanctify the Christian people and to offer sacrifice to God." While acknowledging the importance of the other two *munera* and recognizing the manifold mystery of Christ's ministerial priesthood to which Michael has been ordained, I wish this morning to reflect with you solely upon the *munus sanctificandi* in the light of the Scriptures which we have heard proclaimed.

The fifteenth and sixteenth chapters of the *First Book of Chronicles* recount the festive transfer of the Ark of the Covenant from the house of Obededom the Gittite to the tent which King David had pitched for it in the city which bears his name. It was not, however, the first attempt to move the ark. Three months earlier the ark had been carried on a cart from the house of Abinadab in Kiriathjearim to the region near Obededom's house. But the mission to transport the ark to the City of David had to be aborted for fear of further offending the Lord. For, at one point in that original journey, the oxen pulling the cart stumbled, and the unfortunate Uzzah, seeking to steady the cart, touched the ark and was immediately struck dead. This tragic scene suggests the lack of piety with which King David and his cohort had originally treated the sacred. For, while they themselves had made merry with festive song and dance as they transported the ark, they had failed to provide for the divine worship as God through Moses had prescribed. David later confessed: "we did not care for it in the way that is ordained" (1 Chronicles 15:13). When he resumed the ark's transfer to the City of David some three months later, King David decreed: "No one but the Levites may carry the ark of God, for the Lord chose them to carry the ark of the Lord and to minister to him forever" (1 Chronicles 15:2).

"So the priests and the Levites sanctified themselves to bring up the ark of the Lord, the God of Israel" (1 Chronicles 15:14). They dressed in fine linens, and without touching the ark, they carried it on poles which rested upon their shoulders. Others of the priestly tribe of Levi accompanied the procession with festive song, making music with horns, trumpets, cymbals, harps and lyres. They raised "sounds of joy" (1 Chronicles 15:16) to the Lord, offering a true *sacrificium laudis*. The Lord Himself aided the Levites in their ministry, and in thanksgiving for this grace they offered a sacrifice of seven bulls and seven rams (cf. 1 Chronicles 15:26). Once the ark was placed in the tent pitched for it in the City of David, David and the Levites offered "burnt offerings and peace offerings before God" (1 Chronicles 16:1). Afterwards, in order to provide worthily for the divine worship to be offered "continually morning and evening, according to all that is written in the law of the Lord" (1 Chronicles 16:41), David left in charge "those chosen and expressly named to give thanks to the Lord, for his steadfast love endures for ever" (1 Chronicles 16:41).

The historical account of the ark's festive transfer speaks clearly to us today. It reminds us that our liturgical celebrations are ordained for God's worship and not our own merry making, as it were. When the liturgy is closed in upon itself, that is, when we focus solely upon ourselves and not upon the One whom we worship, it is not life-giving. Right worship, in contrast, leads us beyond ourselves and enables our encounter with the Lord. The priest who faithfully celebrates and truly prays the Mass facilitates this encounter. His celebration should never draw attention to himself. His *ars celebrandi* should be self-effacing, thus allowing the Face of Christ to shine forth. The priest is to be hidden in Christ in order that Christ Himself may be revealed. The sacred vestments and vessels used for the celebration of the Eucharist form an important part of this self-effacing act in a celebration truly worthy of God and in turn truly life-giving for those who participate in it. The priest's own person is hidden, as it were, behind the sacred trappings in order that the faithful's attention not be centered upon his particular personality, but rather that they be led beyond the individual priest towards an encounter with Christ whose presence he ministers to others. In this worthy manner the priest celebrates the Mass not for his own glorification, but rather for the worship of God and the sanctification of His people.

The Gospel account of the Visitation sheds further light upon the priest's sacred anointing. As the Church Fathers understood, the New Testament is the spiritual interpretation of the Old Testament. Saint Luke's Gospel providentially illumines the *First Book of Chronicles*. Specifically, the historical account of the ark's transfer reveals its further depth of spiritual meaning in Mary's journey through the Judaean hill country to the home of Her cousin Elizabeth, the wife of Zechariah to whom the high priest's Temple ministry fell that year. Elizabeth herself came from among the daughters of Aaron (cf. Luke 1:5). Consequently, the home into which Mary entered was a house of the priestly tribe of Levi. Both Mary the Virgin and Elizabeth the sterile had miraculously conceived. Mary was in the first trimester of Her pregnancy while Elizabeth was in her third. Elizabeth bore John the Baptist. With John the prophetic and priestly lines of the Old Testament reached their apex in immediate anticipation of the Divine Word's Incarnation. Mary bore the Son of God Incarnate, the true and eternal High Priest whose unique Sacrifice upon the Cross had been prefigured by the many sacrifices offered by the Levitical priesthood. At Mary's greeting Elizabeth's child leaped for joy. John made merry before the true Ark bearing the Author of the New and Eternal Covenant which the Ark of the Old Covenant, before which David and the ancient Levites had once rejoiced, prophetically symbolized. In John the Jewish priestly order offered fitting worship to God Incarnate, celebrating the advent of the Eternal High Priest.

Deeply moved by this most joyful encounter, Elizabeth humbly inquired: "Why is this granted me, that the mother of my Lord should come to me?" (Luke 1:43). Elizabeth gave voice to the vocational question which all Christian disciples utter and which is particularly found upon the lips of the man whom God through Mother Church calls to Holy Orders. For Mary, the model of the Church *par excellence*, always mediates our encounter with Jesus. Mary, the Mediatrix of all grace, always brings us Jesus, the fruit of Her womb. This encounter with the Mother of Our Lord, through whom the man called to the priesthood meets the Lord Himself, changes his life forever. Indeed, the evangelical mystery of the Visitation lies at the heart of all priestly vocations. It initiates the vocational journey which leads to the man's sacred anointing.

At Mary's greeting Elizabeth was filled with the Holy Spirit. In that instant John received his priestly anointing and leaped for joy. Like John the priest of the New Covenant is also anointed. With the sacred chrism the bishop consecrates the newly ordained priest's hands for the right worship of God and the sanctification of His people. He sacramentally entrusts to the priest the *munus sanctificandi.* That sacred anointing symbolizes liturgically the newly ordained's unique participation in the headship of God's Anointed, Christ Jesus the Eternal High Priest. Thankful for the great gift of the ministerial priesthood, God's people rightly apply to the newly ordained Elizabeth's words to Mary: "Blessed [are you] who believed that there would be a fulfillment of what was spoken to [you] from the Lord" (Luke 1:45). Indeed, Father Pawlowicz, the Church gives abundant thanks that you have trusted in the promises made to you by the Lord and have responded wholeheartedly to His call. We rejoice today in your priesthood and the sacred anointing which you have received to offer sacrifice to God and to be His chosen instrument for the sake of our sanctification. From this day forward may your priestly soul always magnify the Lord among us as you faithfully celebrate the sacred mysteries.

Rome, 25 May 2013
Saturday Memorial of Our Lady

PART TWO

RELIGIOUS LIFE

XI

AMOR MEUS
Faithfully following the Incarnate Word

First Reading: 1 Kings 19:16b, 19-21
Second Reading: Galatians 5:1, 13-18
Gospel: Luke 9:51-62

Today's Gospel speaks of the radical nature of Christian discipleship. Jesus has resolutely determined to journey to Jerusalem. Or, as the Greek text more precisely reads, He has set his face (*autos to prosopon esterisen*) to go to Jerusalem. He looks not back to the tranquility of His Galilean homeland, to that pastoral landscape of rolling green hills surrounding the Sea of Galilee. Rather He has fixed His gaze upon what lies ahead. He looks to Jerusalem. He has consciously begun His ascent to the Cross on Calvary, for His time to be taken up quickly approaches. Along the way others wish to join Him. But are they fully aware of where His path leads?

"I will follow you wherever you go" (Luke 9:57), one such fellow insists. Is he indeed willing to follow Him to Jerusalem, Calvary and the Cross? Jesus responds: "Foxes have holes, and birds of the air have nests; but the Son of man has nowhere to lay his head" (Luke 9:58). Jesus' words had just found immediate confirmation in the Samaritan village's refusal to offer Him hospitality as He made His way to Jerusalem. In 2006, these same evangelical words uttered by a Mexican recalling his mostly forgotten Catholic upbringing proved bitter-sweet for me as I waited at the Cancun airport to board a night flight to Havana on my first trip to Cuba.[1]

The man seated next to me at the gate had prefaced his comments with the question: "What is that white thing around your neck?" "I am a Catholic priest," I explained. Yes, a Catholic priest heading to Communist Cuba. I had no idea what to expect there. Would I be detained at Customs? Would the Father Rector of the seminary be at the airport so late in the night to meet me? Or would I, in fact, have nowhere that night to lay my head? Thankfully, from his childhood the man also recalled Our Lord's words from the Sermon on the Mount: "Look at the birds of the air: they neither sow nor reap nor gather into barns, and yet your heavenly Father feeds them. Are you not of more value than they?" (Matthew 6:26). Yes, these words brought a certain relief. But nonetheless, through this unlikely oracle, the Lord Himself was reminding me that those who answer the call to follow Him must be aware that the Son of Man and His

---

[1] Since the autumn of 2004, I have served as the delegate of the Gregorian University's theology faculty to its affiliate, the *Seminario de San Carlos y San Ambrosio*, in Havana. JCsj

disciples have nowhere to rest their heads—nowhere, that is, but in heaven. For, while the Christian disciple is in the world, he is not to be of it.

Journeying towards Jerusalem Jesus Himself calls another fellow to follow Him. This man would gladly follow Jesus, but only after he has buried his deceased father. To bury the dead is a meritorious act—one of the seven corporal works of mercy. Yet Jesus rebukes him. "Why?" we should ask, for certainly a work of mercy merits no such rebuke. In fact, Jesus' rebuke speaks to us at a deeper level. "Leave the dead to bury their own dead; but as for you, go and proclaim the kingdom of God" (Luke 9:60). The Christian disciple—and here I think especially of the Religious consecrated to Christ's service by the vows of poverty, chastity and obedience—has been called to live and proclaim the *unicum necessarium* which Mary knew at Christ's feet. We are to proclaim the Christ whom we love and adore. The dead are those who do not know Him. They are not only taken up with the mundane, but indeed are overwhelmed by those things which ultimately do not give life. The pursuit of dead things enslaves them. Their addictions drain them of life. Hence, the dead endlessly bury their dead. But the Christian disciple and especially the consecrated Religious live for Christ. This does not mean that we should completely overlook the mundane. After all, we do live in this world and worldly affairs rightly demand our attention—but not our undivided attention which Christ alone merits.[2] Jesus

---

[2] Along these lines SAINT THÉRÈSE OF LISIEUX notes: "I have read how

did not rebuke Martha for doing the good, but rather for trying to take Mary away from the greater good—indeed, the *unicum necessarium*. Martha would have had Mary abandon Life in order to descend among the dead. "Leave the dead to bury their own dead," Jesus could have responded to Martha, "for Mary has chosen to dwell among the living, contemplating the Word of Life."

We Religious must not fear proclaiming Christ. We must not fear making Him present in the world. We must not fear extending His Incarnation by our own visible witness to the Gospel. Indeed, we must resist the temptation to revert back among the dead who simply bury their dead from day to day, that is, we must not allow ourselves to be lost among the mundane, to be not only in the world but to fall back into being of the world. Do we courageously embrace our evangelical mission to go and proclaim the kingdom of God? Perhaps we fear ridicule if we openly speak the Name of Jesus. And yet there is nothing more *natural*, as it were, in the eyes of the faithful and even of the non-believer than when a Religious or a priest speaks of Christ Jesus and His Gospel. Truly, the words of Scripture ought to be our native tongue.

On His way to Jerusalem, Jesus calls a third individual

---

the Israelites built the walls of Jerusalem, working with one hand and holding a sword in the other. This is what we must do: never give ourselves over entirely to our tasks," *St. Thérèse of Lisieux: Her Last Conversations*, trans. JOHN CLARKE, O.C.D. (Washington, D.C.: ICS Publications, 1977), p. 96.

who responds to Christ's call as Elisha had initially responded to the call of Elijah. Although eager to follow Jesus, he wishes first to bid his family farewell. In reply Jesus admonishes him: "No one who puts his hand to the plow and looks back is fit for the kingdom of God" (Luke 9:62). Here the words of Saint Paul to the Philippians come immediately to mind. "Indeed," Saint Paul writes, "I count everything as loss because of the surpassing worth of knowing Christ Jesus my Lord. For his sake I have suffered the loss of all things, and count them as refuse, in order that I may gain Christ and be found in him....[F]orgetting what lies behind and straining forward to what lies ahead, I press on toward the goal for the prize of the upward call of God in Christ Jesus" (Philippians 3:8-9a, 13-14). The Apostle has unflinchingly set his hand to the plow and steadily keeps his gaze fixed squarely upon Christ Jesus. If we are to be Jesus' faithful disciples, then we, too, must steadfastly fix our gaze upon Christ's Holy Face.[3] For, all else is secondary and could well prove a distraction in our wholehearted service of the Lord.

---

[3] In speaking of her own devotion to the Holy Face, SAINT THÉRÈSE OF LISIEUX relates: "These words of Isaias: 'Who has believed our report?...There is no beauty in him, no comeliness, etc.,' have made the whole foundation of my devotion to the Holy Face, or, to express it better, the foundation of all my piety. I, too, have desired to be without beauty, alone in treading the winepress, unknown to everyone," *St. Thérèse of Lisieux: Her Last Conversations*, trans. JOHN CLARKE, O.C.D. (Washington, D.C.: ICS Publications, 1977), p. 135.

Like Saint Paul, Venerable Jeanne Chézard de Matel,[4] your Mother Foundress, gave herself entirely over to the Lord. She enjoyed an intimate relationship with Jesus. Her *Spiritual Journal* reveals the depths of their loving mystical exchanges. Her contemplative vision was clearly focused on Christ. She experienced Him in the depths of mystical prayer, she met Him in Sacred Scripture, and she adored Him in the Blessed Sacrament. Her one love—the *amor meus* of your emblem—was the Incarnate Word. When at prayer one evening in the Jesuit college church of Roanne, she beheld "a Crown of Thorns within which was [His] Name, *Jesus*. Above it, there was a heart with the words *Amor meus* written there. [Jesus] said to [her]: 'My daughter, my Name is as oil poured out. A number of daughters will be attracted to this Order by the sweetness of this Name. Have It placed on the red scapular that you saw in this vision so that I may repose upon the breast of my faithful spouses. While I was mortal, I justly complained that the foxes have their dens and the birds their nests, but that I had no place whereon to place my head. Let Me repose upon your breasts.'"[5] Venerable

---

[4] JEANNE CHÉZARD DE MATEL was born on 6 November 1596 in Roanne, and died on 11 September 1670 in Paris. On 2 July 1625, the feast of the Visitation, she began living in community with two companions. This date marks the beginning of the Order of the Religious Sisters of the Incarnate Word and Blessed Sacrament. The Order's foundation in Houston, Texas, dates from 1873.

[5] JEANNE CHÉZARD DE MATEL, *Autobiographic Life*, Complete Works, vol. 1 (Rome, 1993), p. 142.

Jeanne obediently embraced Christ's call that she and her daughters bear His Name upon their breast and that they be clothed in the red and white of His Passion[6]—sharing "his sufferings, becoming like him in his death, that if possible [she and you, her daughters,] may attain the resurrection from the dead" (Philippians 3:10-11). Behold how even here in the Motherhouse chapel the symbols of the Paschal Mystery depicted in the stained-glass windows surround you.

---

[6] Cf. Ibid., pp. 134-136: "...On January 15, 1625, while at Mass offered by Rev. Father Coton [S.J.] in the small chapel of the College of Roanne, You elevated my spirit by a sublime suspension during which You appeared to me wearing a threadbare and somewhat faded purple mantle. This symbolized for me the one given to You in derision together with the Crown of Thorns and a reed for a scepter while You were mocked by shouts: *Ave rex Judeorum, Hail, King of the Jews*. You made my soul your tabernacle and my heart your throne, giving me to understand that You wanted the daughters of your Order to wear a red mantel. ... A few months later, You appeared to me wearing a white robe and said to me: 'I am He who is the *candidus et rubicundus, white and red* Spouse, chosen above all mankind and all the Angels; I am the predestined Son of God. I wish to invest the daughters of my Order with this white of innocence and red of charity. These are my colors and my vesture....Tell them, my daughter, to weep over the death of the King of Love; I, the Sovereign, am He. I have clothed them with my own Blood. Let them be my spouses of blood, but a blood that eternally preserves its brilliance and vivid color so as to fortify them in their struggle along life's way and gladden them with peace at its end. Let their white robe honor the one given Me by Herod, and their [red] mantle honor the one presented to Me by Pilate. Upon their scapular, represent my Cross through the Blood of which I have pacified heaven and earth.'"

Venerable Jeanne de Matel's charism is first and fore-most a contemplative charism. It is a charism to contemplate Christ, to live a life completely consecrated to the Incarnate Word. This sacred charism is yours. In the coming days you will prayerfully seek to renew her God-given charism within you as you make your annual retreat. You will meditate upon Jesus' words—the Word of God so precious to your Foundress who received the grace to understand without previous study the Latin of the Vulgate. You will pray before Christ's Real Presence among us in the Blessed Sacrament exposed upon the altar. You have committed yourselves dur-ing those hours of adoration to pray especially for priestly and Religious vocations. May your Mother Foundress' own experience in Eucharistic Adoration inspire you. For, it was during such adoration on 23 June 1625 that Our Lord spoke to Venerable Jeanne in words echoing Saint Augustine of Hippo, *amor meus pondus meum*,[7] espousing her to Himself as His bride, the bride of the Lamb.[8] As you pray before the Blessed Sacrament for vocations, renew your own consecra-tion. Enter more deeply into your own spousal union with Jesus. May today's Gospel likewise guide your week-long prayer. For, Christian discipleship in general, the Religious life in particular and above all an Order dedicated to the In-carnate Word and Blessed Sacrament are characterized by a singular love for Jesus in both Word and Sacrament in the

---

[7] AUGUSTINE OF HIPPO, *Confessions* 13.9.10: "What draws me to my rest-ing place (literally, my weight) is my love."

[8] Cf. JEANNE CHÉZARD DE MATEL, *Autobiographic Life*, p. 143.

Church. The more you radiate this singular love—that is, the more other women behold the lived reality of the words *amor meus* embroidered upon your scapular—the more your consecration to the *unicum necessarium* will draw others to join you so that the Incarnate Word may be praised both now and forever more. Amen.

Houston, 27 June 2010
The Thirteenth Sunday of Ordinary Time

XII

THE MYSTERY OF THE LAMB
Wounded, I will never cease to love

Reading: Hebrews 3:7-14

This evening we have been brought together by the mystery of the Lamb whose death upon the Cross has taken away our sins. In an especial way this mystery is the charism of the Community of the Lamb. I take a great risk this evening in speaking to you about the community's charism. For, I venture to speak of it in the presence of Little Sister Marie, the community's Foundress. Nonetheless, despite the notable risk, I still wish to recall with you the story of Little Sister Marie's experience out of which the community's charism arose. But first, by way of introduction, I should note that earlier today I was reflecting with one of you from the Catholic Studies program present in the chapel this evening about the mystery of suffering. "Why is there suffering?", he asked me with anguish, wondering then immediately if the faithful Christian should even ask such a question. "Is it right for us to ask the question 'why?'", the seminarian humbly pondered. "Yes, of course, it is," I said in reply. I explained that, in fact, it was while asking that very question that the Community of the Lamb was born.

On the night of September 13th, 1975, the vigil of the Feast of the Triumph of the Cross, Little Sister Marie gathered together with others in prayer. They prayed throughout the night, asking the Lord, "Why does evil exist? Why do people continue to suffer in our world?" "Why, Lord, why?", they implored. The Lord responded to them in the words of Saint Paul's *Letter to the Ephesians*: "But now in Christ Jesus you who once were far off have been brought near in the blood of Christ. For he is our peace, who has made us both one, and has broken down the dividing wall of hostility, by abolishing in his flesh the law of commandments and ordinances, that he might create in himself one new man in place of the two, so making peace, and might reconcile us both to God in one body through the cross, thereby bringing the hostility to an end" (Ephesians 2:13-16). Jesus did not simply tell Little Sister Marie and the others, "I have heard your prayer. By tomorrow morning, I will have removed all evil and suffering from the world." Rather, He reminded them that He Himself has entered into our suffering. He, who is our God, has embraced our suffering in His humanity. He has taken upon Himself and indeed into Himself all hatred and evil, and by that means, He has triumphed over it. This is the mystery of the Cross in which Saint John the Evangelist beholds Christ's glorious exaltation. By means of love, a crucified love, Christ has conquered hatred and evil, triumphing over even death itself.

The motto of the Community of the Lamb is: "Wounded, I will never cease to love." This saying succinctly sums up the community's charism. But to understand how wounded love triumphs, we must turn our gaze to Christ Crucified. In every chapel of the Community of the Lamb hangs the *San Damiano* Cross. Look at this Cross. Notice that the Crucified Christ bears all five wounds of His passion. His hands, feet and side are pierced. Recall that Christ Jesus received the wound in His side—His fifth and final wound—only after He had died. Yet here upon this Cross, His eyes are open. He is not the dead Christ, but rather the Risen Lord Jesus Crucified. Although wounded, He has not ceased to love us. Death has not had the final word. Rather, Christ's wounded love has triumphed over sin and death. In Him love proves victorious.

The Risen Lord Jesus Crucified continues to bear in His glorified body the open wounds of His passion not as a sign of defeat, but rather as a sign of victory—the victory of Divine Love Incarnate which His death mysteriously reveals. Even though wounded—indeed, mortally wounded—Jesus has never ceased to love us. When we gaze upon the Risen Lord Jesus Crucified, we find the answer to the question why we suffer. We are reminded of that love than which there is no greater—that sacrificial love which alone triumphs over all hatred, evil, sin and death. From the Cross, Christ reveals to us that "greater love has no man than this, that a man lay down his life for his friends" (John 15:13). Jesus calls each one of us to live this love as well—to suffer lovingly for the sake of the other and his salvation.

But let us not forget that, when we suffer in life, we have a choice. We can allow our hearts to be hardened by anger and hatred. We can allow bitterness to invade us and

121

to form within us "an evil, unbelieving heart, leading [us] to fall away from the living God" (Hebrews 3:12). Indeed, we can be "hardened by the deceitfulness of sin" (Hebrews 3:13). Wounded, we can all too easily cease to love. Thus, no longer loving, we would be most truly dead. Or we can choose to love. Although wounded, we can choose never to stop loving. Humanly speaking, such love is impossible. Wounded, we can only continue to love with the help of God's grace. The Lord Himself comes then and takes from us hearts hardened by anger and hatred, and places within us His own Heart of flesh—a wounded Heart which has never ceased to love. His Heart has been pierced and ripped open so that we may enter into It and rest therein. Only then, dwelling within the pierced Heart of Christ, can we learn to love one another as He has loved us from the Cross. Such love is a grace, the gift of God freely given. In our Eucharistic celebration this evening, we give thanks to God the Father through His Crucified and Risen Son for this gift of wounded love victorious.

Rome, 13 January 2011

XIII

THE HOLY HOUSE
AND THE HOLY HABIT
Putting on Christ in the service of the Gospel

Gospel: Luke 1:26-38

As the last crusaders left the Holy Land towards the end of the thirteenth century, they carefully dismantled Our Lady's house at Nazareth brick by brick and brought that precious relic back with them to Europe. The dwelling's three walls had enclosed a stone grotto. Today above that Nazarene grotto stands the Basilica of the Annunciation. But those three walls have been reassembled within the sanctuary of this magnificent church in Loreto. The crusaders had originally brought the bricks of Our Lady's house to Dalmatia—the coastal region of modern-day Croatia. But the Angelini family of Loreto paid for the relic's reconstruction here on the opposite shore of the Adriatic Sea. While the medieval receipt for that reconstruction still exists, a medieval legend gives credit for the Holy House's final transfer not to the Angelini, but rather to the *angeli*—God's holy angels. In contrast to the legend, however, the historical account of the Holy House's relocation allows us to say with conviction that the Holy House of Loreto is indeed the Holy House of Nazareth where the Divine Word became flesh and first dwelt among us. Within these walls the Divine Word clothed Himself with our humanity. He became incarnate. Inseparably and indivisibly, yet without confusion or mixture did He unite our humanity to His divinity in His one divine Person. The Son of God truly became the man Jesus Christ, speaking His divine *ego*—His divine "I"—with a human voice and loving us divinely with a human Heart. The Divine Word, however, did not embark upon His redemptive mission without first enlisting our cooperation. He sent before Himself the Archangel Gabriel to announce to the Virgin Mary at Her home in Nazareth the singular mission which was to be Hers, and only at Mary's freely uttered *fiat* did the Word become flesh.

An earlier clothing, the Immaculate Conception of the Blessed Virgin Mary, had preceded and indeed prepared the way for the incarnate clothing of the Divine Word. In creating the woman who would be His own Mother, God preserved Mary from the stain of Original Sin. He clothed Her with the sun, placed the moon under Her feet and crowned Her with twelve stars at the dawn of Her existence. From the beginning the fullness of His grace penetrated into the very depths of Her being. For, from Her immaculate flesh, He intended to form His own sinless humanity. In virtue of Her vocation to be the Mother of God, Mary shared by means of anticipation in Her Son's universal redemption. Full of grace, She enjoyed perfect freedom. No sin ever impaired Her wholehearted response to God's call. She alone among our entire race could cooperate graciously and freely with the divine plan for our salvation. At Her yes the Divine Word became flesh within the walls of the Holy House of Nazareth now venerated at Loreto. Mary's immaculate clothing providentially enabled the Divine Word's incarnate clothing for the sake of our salvation.

God clothed both Our Lady with His grace at Her Conception and Himself in our humanity at His Incarnation for the sake of mission. Our Lord and Our Lady obediently embraced that redemptive mission. The Lord's humble handmaid proclaimed: "Let it be to me according to your word" (Luke 1:38). Christ Jesus, the Divine Word Incarnate, having emptied Himself and taken on the form of a slave, being found in the likeness of men, "humbled himself and became obedient unto death, even death on a cross" (Philippians 2:8). These sacred clothings speak to us most clearly of obedience and mission. Indeed, they attest to the obedience of all the baptized faithful to the Father's will for the sake of mission in the world redeemed by His Son. At their baptism all Christians have become a new creation and clothed themselves in Christ. By means of an intensified consecration, Religious seek to live with singular devotion their baptismal vocation. To that end they are clothed with a distinct garment as a visible sign of their mission embraced in obedience to God within the Church for the sake of furthering Christ's salvific mission in the world. Today we celebrate such a religious clothing in the singular setting of the Holy House of Loreto wherein the Immaculate Virgin conceived the Divine Word made man.

Today Megan Crain and Sarah DeCock receive the habit

of the Handmaids of the Heart of Jesus. The investiture ritual reminds us that the habit is "a sign of [their] total consecration to Christ." As the new novices don their religious habits for the first time, they also witness before us to that tremendous day when the dead shall rise from their graves and the just will be clothed in immortal glory. How eloquently the habit symbolizes the twofold nature of the religious life—a life consecrated to Christ in this world, which points beyond this world to that life with Christ in the world to come. Each particular element of the habit, moreover, specifically symbolizes a distinct aspect of the religious life to which the novice hopes one day to vow herself. The tunic sets her apart from this world's vanities for a life of poverty with Christ poor. The veil distinguishes her as one betrothed in chastity to Christ the Bridegroom. The belt reminds her of the obedience which frees her to respond wholeheartedly to Christ's commands and the Holy Spirit's inspirations. The scapular marks her as the Lord's humble handmaid in imitation of the Blessed Virgin Mary. Finally, the rosary constantly at her side recalls the life of continuous prayer which pertains to all Christians but is particularly her own. In sum the habit witnesses visibly to that contemplative life lived in humble service which so notably characterizes the Handmaids of the Heart of Jesus.

Megan and Sarah, as you wear the religious habit faithfully, realize that by this visible sign you are witnessing always to Christ before the world—a world particularly "sensitive to the language of signs" (cf. JOHN PAUL II, *Vita Consecrata* § 25). You are boldly proclaiming to all your availability to serve, your desire to preach the Gospel at all times, and your willingness to be inconvenienced, as it were, for the sake of those in spiritual and material need. By wearing the habit faithfully, you demonstrate that your humble service is not something that you yourselves wish to regulate or control. Rather, in your continual docility to God's will which the habit reveals, you remain ever open to divine providence, to serve when God would have you serve, where God would have you serve and how God would have you serve. As we have already noted, your habit conforms you to the poor Christ. It is the outward sign of one who has indeed abandoned all things and followed Him. By wearing the habit faithfully you witness before the world that Christ Jesus alone is your heart's treasure. The habit is also a discipline which will aid you in your weakness to keep your eyes fixed solely upon Our Lord. It will be a constant reminder to you of your call and consecration. It will serve to deter the Old Eve within you from taking you down paths which would lead you away from Christ. Finally, wearing the religious habit faithfully attests to your life within the Church. It witnesses to your obedience and your ecclesial mission in accord with Blessed Pope John Paul II,[1] who, in his Post-Synodal Apostolic Exhortation on the Consecrated Life, strongly recommended that men and women religious wear their proper habit (cf. JOHN PAUL II, *Vita Consecrata* § 25). While the habit does not make the monk, the faithful monk is not to be found without his habit. When worn faithfully the religious

---

[1] On 27 April 2014, Pope Francis canonized Pope John Paul II.

habit (and for that matter, the clerical garb of priests) harmoniously expresses exteriorly an interior life of continual conversion and consecration, a life docile to the Spirit, available for mission, given over completely to Christ and freed in obedience for His faithful service within the Church for the sake of the world's salvation.

Megan and Sarah, put on Christ. Clothe yourselves in His humility. Turn to Our Lady, the Lord's humble handmaid, and imitate Her whom God clothed in His grace. On this day of your clothing with the holy habit, make your own the words which Mary spoke in the Holy House when, as She was overshadowed by the Holy Spirit, the Divine Word clothed Himself with our human nature formed from Her immaculate flesh: "Behold, I am the handmaid of the Lord; let it be to me according to your word" (Luke 1:38).

Loreto, 1 July 2013

PART THREE

THE PASCHAL MYSTERY

XIV

SAINT CLEMENT OF ROME, LENT 2010
Presiding in love

Reading: Daniel 9:4-10
Psalm 78 (79)
Gospel: Luke 6:36-38

The relics of two Church Fathers lie beneath the Basilica altar. The urn contains the earthly remains of Saint Clement of Rome and Saint Ignatius of Antioch. Each in his respective see was a successor of Saint Peter. Each also attests to the primacy of the Church of Rome consecrated in the blood of Peter and Paul's final witness—a primacy which Rome uniquely exercises in the Church Universal. At the close of the first Christian century while the Apostle John still lived and the apostolic witness recorded in what would become the New Testament canon was still being written down, Clement in the name of the Roman Church fraternally and indeed authoritatively admonished the Church suffering schism at Corinth. Some fourteen years later, Ignatius acknowledged that the Church of Rome, having been instructed in the faith by Peter and Paul, taught others in an unparalleled fashion (cf. IGNATIUS OF ANTIOCH, *Letter to the Romans*, 3.1). Although he himself had heard John preach in Asia Minor and had succeeded Peter at Antioch, Ignatius did not presume to command the Roman Church. Rather he extolled her in the most exalted terms. He greeted her as "the Church that has found mercy in the transcendent Majesty of the Most High Father and of Jesus Christ, His only Son…; a church worthy of God, worthy of success, worthy of sanctification, and presiding in love, maintaining the law of Christ, and bearer of the Father's name" (IGNATIUS OF ANTIOCH, *Letter to the Romans*, preface).[1] He concluded that her saints "imperturbably enjoy the full measure of God's grace and have every foreign stain filtered out of them" (Ibid.).

Ignatius' salutation highlighting Rome's presidency in love is well known. But what exactly does it mean (1) *to preside* and (2) *in love*? Firstly, the Greek verb *to preside* (*prokathemai*) has a juridical meaning. Plato uses the verb to identify the activities of the sovereign municipal body which convokes and dissolves institutional assemblies (cf. PLATO, *Laws*, VI.758d). Found in Aristotle's *Politics* (VI.1322^{b}14) the verb refers to the administrative oversight of municipal goods. This municipal supervision is exercised by "a body which convenes the supreme authority in the State"; its members

---

[1] IGNATIUS OF ANTIOCH, "Ignatius to the Romans," *The Epistles of St. Clement of Rome and St. Ignatius of Antioch*, Ancient Christian Writers, vol. 1, trans. JAMES A. KLEIST, SJ (Westminster: The Newman Bookshop, 1946), p. 80.

hold "the chief political offices" (ARISTOTLE, *Politics* VI.1322[b]15-17).[2] Writing to the Magnesians, Ignatius employs this same Greek verb to describe the role of the bishop who presides in the place of God over the local church (cf. IGNATIUS OF ANTIOCH, *Letter to the Magnesians*, 6.1). As for the Greek word *agape*, that is, love, it denotes in ancient Christian usage much more than mere affection or charitable giving. It stands as a synonym for the Eucharist and the ecclesial communion which the Sacrament effects (cf. IGNATIUS OF ANTIOCH, *Letter to the Romans*, 7.3). Hence, the Church of Rome solicitously oversees or governs the ecclesial communion which unites all the Christian faithful together in love. This unique mission of service is a grace. More precisely, it is a share in the singular grace which Peter first received at Caesarea Philippi and which the Risen Christ later confirmed at the Sea of Galilee. This grace against which "the powers of death shall not prevail" (Matthew 16:18) filters out every foreign stain. It assures fidelity to God's commandments, and is an infallible expression of the new covenant which God has established with His People in Christ Jesus.

The prophet Daniel attests that the Lord, the great and awesome God, keeps His merciful covenant towards those who love Him and observe His commandments (cf. Daniel 9:4b). But Daniel likewise laments the pitiable state of an ex-

---

[2] ARISTOTLE, *The Complete Works of Aristotle*, Revised Oxford Translation, vol. 2, ed. JONATHAN BARNES (Princeton: Princeton University Press, 1985), p. 2099.

iled Israel which had sinned, rebelled and paid no heed to the Lord's commands. The prophet is confident, nonetheless, that the Lord will not abandon His chosen people, "for," as Saint Paul will later attest, "the gifts and the call of God are irrevocable" (Romans 11:29). Indeed, far from abandoning His people, the God of Israel sent them His only-begotten Son as the seed of Abraham conceived in the Virgin Mother's womb. In Christ Jesus, the Father mercifully calls fallen humanity back to Himself. Through Baptism and the Eucharist, we become members of Christ's ecclesial Body wherein we are restored to communion with our heavenly Father. The Universal Church over which Rome lovingly presides is holy and without blemish because she is Christ's Body, animated by His Spirit and sanctified by His Sacraments. Yet she, like the chosen but exiled Israel, paradoxically stands "always in need of purification" (Vatican II, *Lumen Gentium* § 8) because in virtue of her mission to be the locus of humanity's reconciliation with the Father in Christ she clasps sinners to her bosom (cf. Ibid.).

As the prophet Daniel acknowledges, holiness is on the Lord's side. Christ expresses His righteousness in the compassion which He bears for sinners, in particular for the sinful members of His Body the Church. As a pilgrim people comprised of sinners, the Church must continually walk upon the path of penance and renewal until the day we enter into our heavenly fatherland. Along this gracious path of conversion, we are divinized, that is, made to be like God. To this end Christ exhorts us to "be merciful, even as [our] Father is merciful" (Luke 6:36). Such mercy consists in embracing sinners, praying for our persecutors and loving our enemies in imitation of Jesus, Divine Mercy Incarnate, who forgave His executioners from the Cross. In such mercy consists the divine perfection to which we are called as the sons and daughters of our heavenly Father (cf. Matthew 5:44-45, 48).

In sum, ecclesial communion rightly includes not only the saint, but also the sinner. The figure of Peter powerfully attests to this truth. At Caesarea Philippi Christ did not entrust the keys of the Kingdom to the young innocent Saint John who one day would stand faithfully with His Mother Mary at the foot of His Cross. Rather, He entrusted the keys to the one who would thrice deny knowing Him in His greatest hour of need. Thus "it was provided," Saint Optatus of Milevis wisely observes, "that the sinner should open [the gates of heaven] to the innocent, so that the innocent would not turn the keys against sinners" (OPTATUS OF MILEVIS, *Against the Donatists*, VII.3).[3] In the papal insignia the tiara rests upon these keys which bind in order to forgive. These ancient keys rather than the medieval tiara represent the true glory of the Roman Church which measures with the measure of Peter, the passiontide apostate reconciled in mercy and martyred for love. Here at Rome the Catholic Church first recognized the possibility of a second repentance for serious sin committed after Baptism. In antiquity it was the Church of Rome and those in communion with her who op-

---

[3] OPTATUS OF MILEVIS, *Optatus: Against the Donatists*, Translated Texts for Historians, vol. 27, trans. MARK EDWARDS (Liverpool: Liverpool Press University, 1997), p. 141.

posed the rigorism of the Montantists, Novantianists and Donatists. Even in our own day, while condemning without compromise the evil of sin, especially those sins committed against the young and the vulnerable, the Successor of Saint Peter demonstrates his loving concern for each particular Church suffering on account of her members' sins. Presiding in love, Pope Benedict XVI exhorts us all to do penance for the sake of the Church's renewal. May our penances and prayers offered this Lent from the heart of the Eternal City be a worthy expression of the Father's mercy present in "good measure, pressed down, shaken together [and] running over" (Luke 6:38) in the Church of Rome which presides in love.

Rome, 1 March 2010
The Second Monday of Lent

XV

SAINT CLEMENT OF ROME, LENT 2011
Living Christian unity

Reading: Daniel 9:4-10
Psalm 78 (79)
Gospel: Luke 6:36-38

In the station-church San Clemente, the Universal Church breathes deeply with both lungs. Beneath the altar lie the relics of a western and an eastern bishop: Saint Clement of Rome and Saint Ignatius of Antioch. Both had succeeded Saint Peter in their respective sees. Clement exercised the Petrine primacy in Rome whose presidency in love Ignatius writing from Asia Minor would later praise. According to an ancient tradition, Clement suffered exile and martyrdom in Asia Minor at the beginning of the second Christian century. With an anchor tied around his neck, he was reportedly flung into the Black Sea. Ignatius was to follow Clement's path, but in reverse. Arrested in Antioch he was brought forcibly to Rome and fed to wild beasts whose jaws ground his body like wheat. What the lions did not consume we venerate in this church. But for almost eight centuries, Clement's relics rested either submerged beneath the sea or buried in its immediate vicinity. They remained there until discovered by a Greek priest named Constantine better known to us as Saint Methodius' equally saintly sibling Cyril. Saint Cyril retrieved the Pontiff's relics. He carried them from the Crimea to Moravia and eventually brought them to Rome. He, along with his brother, came to the Eternal City in the year 867 in order to seek papal approval for the Slavonic liturgy which, even though playing a pivotal role in the central European Slavs' evangelization, had met with opposition from the western clergy. While in Rome the saintly brothers entrusted Saint Clement's relics to Pope Adrian II who eventually did solemnly sanction the Slavonic rites. The Roman Pontiff favored liturgical diversity for the sake of ecclesial unity, providing an early medieval precedent for contemporary papal practice.[1] During his Roman sojourn, Constantine received the monastic habit and took the name Cyril. The Greek monk, however, was never to leave Rome. For, fifty days later he died and was buried in the fourth-century church dedicated to Saint Clement which lies below our feet. San Clemente's venerable history reveals an ancient unity. For many centuries within these walls, the Christian East and West have fraternally embraced.

Commenting upon Jesus' high-priestly prayer *ut unum sint*—that His disciples be one—, Pope Benedict XVI writes in *Jesus of Nazareth*, part two, that "[u]nity does not come

---

[1] Cf. POPE BENEDICT XVI, Motu Proprio *Summorum Pontificum*, 7 July 2007.

from the world: on the basis of the world's own efforts, it is impossible. The world's own efforts lead to disunion, as we can all see. Inasmuch as the world is operative in the Church, in Christianity, it leads to schisms. Unity can only come from the Father through the Son".[2] In today's first reading the prophet Daniel laments how the world has infiltrated the people of Israel whom he reproaches for their disobedience, treachery and rebellion. Their worldliness has resulted in exile and division. But despite the people's infidelity, God remains merciful, just, compassionate and forgiving. It is His mercy alone which restores Israel. In this light, we can see how the ecclesial unity, to which the ecumenical drama of San Clemente so powerfully attests, is nothing other than the fruit of God's mercy and grace. The Father grants the gift of ecclesial unity through the prayer of Jesus who Peter confesses to be "the Son of the living God" (Matthew 16:16). As Pope Benedict instructs, future ecclesial unity will be grounded upon this faith in the Son which Peter professes not only at Caesarea Philippi but also at the synagogue in Capernaum where in the Twelve's name the Chief Apostle loyally declares Jesus to be "the Holy One of God" (John 6:69). At Caesarea Philippi Jesus acknowledged that "flesh and blood [had] not revealed this to [Peter], but [His] Father who is in heaven" (Matthew 16: 17). In sum, Peter's profession of faith, which grounds the Church's unity, is the fruit of the Father's mercy.

---

[2] JOSEPH RATZINGER/ POPE BENEDICT XVI, *Jesus of Nazareth: Holy Week* (San Francisco: Ignatius Press, 2011), p. 95.

JOSEPH CAROLA, SJ

To be merciful as our Father is merciful, then, is to labor graciously for such unity among ourselves and all the baptized faithful, to enter into the spirit of forgiveness which breaks down the walls of division, to live the visible catholic unity which the eastern and western saints of San Clemente enjoyed on earth and celebrate in heaven. To that end, fearing neither Saint Cyril's exhausting labors, the Apostolic Fathers' martyrdoms nor Saint Peter's final witness in Nero's circus on the Vatican hill, we measure with the measure of Peter and profess in word and deed the fullness of our Catholic faith. With Peter and his Successor before a world increasingly more hostile to Christ's Gospel, may our tongues unceasingly proclaim to the glory of God the Father: Jesus Christ is Lord (cf. Philippians 2:11).

Rome, 21 March 2011
The Second Monday of Lent

XVI

SAINT CLEMENT OF ROME, LENT 2013
Chastening the body to heal the soul

Reading: *Daniel 9:4-10*
Psalm 78 (79)
Gospel: *Luke 6:36-38*

The new English translation of the *Collect* for the second Monday of Lent faithfully conveys the spiritual depths of the Latin text. Recall the words which we have prayed: "O God, who have taught us to chasten our bodies for the healing of our souls, enable us ... to abstain from all sins and strengthen our hearts to carry out your loving commands" (*The Roman Missal*, 3rd edition, 2011). God's loving commands—*pietatis mandata*—call us to continence, that is, to the self-mastery of our bodies for the right ordering of our souls.

Following the threefold anthropological division found in Saint Paul's *First Letter to the Thessalonians*, the Church Fathers understand man to be composed of spirit, soul and body (cf. 1 Thessalonians 5:23). The soul itself consists of two further parts: its higher rational faculties and its lower instinctual passions. When reason reigns over the passions, the human soul is rightly ordered to those spiritual goods which are above. But when the passions dominate, the human soul is dragged down towards those base attractions which weary and disturb, leading man away from God. To chasten our bodies means to order our passions according to right reason. This ordering results in the savoring of spiritual goods and ultimately in the contemplation of God who has created us for Himself and in whom alone our hearts find rest. On this account, both today's *Prayer over the Offerings* and the *Prayer after Communion* speak respectively of being set free from worldly attractions and cleansed of wrongdoing in order to serve the heavenly mysteries and to inherit the joy of heaven. Such moral cleansing and spiritual liberation require God's grace. For this reason we pray that God both enable us to abstain from all sins and strengthen us to fulfill His commands.

In the tenth book of his *Confessions*, Saint Augustine of Hippo adverts to this spiritual dynamic. He recognizes both the call to continence, that is, the call to control our bodily desires, and the need of God's grace to achieve that end. In the pursuit of continence, Augustine humbly acknowledges before the Lord: "There can be no hope for me except in your great mercy. ... Give me the grace to do as you command, and command me to do what you will" (AUGUSTINE OF HIPPO, *Confessions* 10.29)![1] God commands us to control

---

[1] AUGUSTINE OF HIPPO, *Confessions*, trans. R. S. PINE-COFFIN (New York: Penguin Books, 1961), p. 233.

our bodily desires for the sake of our spiritual wellbeing. "Truly it is by continence," Augustine observes, "that we are made as one and regain that unity of self which we lost by falling apart in the search for a variety of pleasures" (Ibid.). The unchaste body pursues idolatrous loves placed on par with that love owed to God alone. Thus it violates the First Commandment by having other gods before Him. Continence casts out such idolatry from the temple of the human body. For, chastening the body fractured by a multitude of base pleasures restores to the soul that pure love and single-heartedness which sees God and adores Him alone.

Concluding his confession, Augustine ecstatically implores: "O Love ever burning, never quenched! O Charity, my God, set me on fire with your love! You command me to be continent. Give me the grace to do as you command, and command me to do what you will" (Ibid.)! Similarly, at the beginning of this Holy Mass, we have prayed: "O God, who have taught us to chasten our bodies for the healing of our souls, enable us ... to abstain from all sins and strengthen our hearts to carry out your loving commands."

Rome, 25 February 2013
The Second Monday of Lent

XVII

SAINT CLEMENT OF ROME, LENT 2014
Yearning for God like the deer for running streams

Reading: Daniel 9:4-10
Psalm 78 (79)
Gospel: Luke 6:36-38

At the center of the twelfth-century mosaic adorning the San Clemente apse stands the Cross of Christ revealed as the Tree of Life. The *lignum vitae* arises from a lush acanthus plant whose vine sprawls across the entire apse. The Latin inscription at the base of the apse mosaic reads: "We have likened the Church of Christ to this vine; the Law made it wither but the Cross made it bloom." Beneath the tree of life and its blooming branches flow the four rivers of Eden. Two deer drink from its running streams. In the bush above those streams stands a third deer contending with a serpent. Even though Saint Patrick may have driven the serpents out of Ireland, at San Clemente a snake remains in the Irish Dominicans' grass.

The story of the deer and the serpent depicted in the apse mosaic comes from antiquity. In his monumental first-century study, *Naturalis Historia*, Pliny the Elder observes that deer fight with serpents. "They seek out the serpents' dens and by the breath of their nostrils they drive them out despite their resistance" (PLINY THE ELDER, *Naturalis Historia* 8.32.118).[1] In sixth-century Calabria, Cassiodorus applied Pliny's zoological science to his exegesis of the first verse of Psalm forty-two: "Like the deer that yearns for running streams, so my soul is yearning for you, my God" (Psalm 42:1). Each year on this second Monday of Lent we begin our Morning Prayer with that very psalm. Cassiodorus explains that the deer "attracts snakes with its nostrils; when it has devoured them, the seething poison impels it to hasten with all speed to the water-fountain, for it loves to get its fill of the purest sweet water" (CASSIODORUS, *Expositio in psalmo* 41.2 (CCL 97, 380)).[2] So it likewise is with Christ's faithful. As Cassiodorus continues: "[W]hen we imbibe the poisons of the ancient serpent, and we are feverish through his torches, we may there and then hasten to the fount of divine mercy. Thus the sickness contracted by the venom of sin is overcome by the purity of this most sweet drink."[3] It is Christ the Lord, Cassiodorus concludes, who "is the Fount of water from which flows all that refreshes

---

[1] PLINE L'ANCIEN, *Histoire Naturelle*, Livre VIII, ed. A ERNOUT (Paris : Société d'Edition « Les Belles Lettres », 1952), p. 64.

[2] CASSIODORUS, *Explanation of the Psalms*, vol. I (Psalms 1-51 (50)), trans. P. G. WALSH (New York: Paulist Press, 1990), p. 416.

[3] Ibid.

us."[4] Cassiodorus' sixth-century exegesis eventually found its way into the twelfth-century *Glossa Ordinaria*—a vast patristic scriptural commentary contemporaneous with San Clemente's magnificent apse mosaic.

The deer and the serpent placed at the base of the apse mosaic Cross symbolize Original Sin whose seething poison finds its antidote in the waters of Baptism. In Adam all men have sinned and stand justly condemned. Our first parents' sin, which we have contracted, has been compounded by the actual sins, which we ourselves have committed. On this account the prophet Daniel rightly laments: "We have sinned and done wrong and acted wickedly and rebelled, turning aside from thy commandments and ordinances" (Daniel 9:5). Given our sins both original and actual, we are like prisoners "doomed to die" (Psalm 79:11). The Old Law only served to convict us of sin. It could not redeem us from it. But the Just Judge is compassionate and forgiving. Having heard our cry for deliverance, God sent His only-begotten Son as an expiation for our sins. From the wounded side of the Crucified Christ flow the blood and water in which we are cleansed. Christ's grace restores us. Withering no longer we bloom.

Who of us, however, cannot lament that the occasional snake still gets into the grass? Baptized and forgiven we recognize our continual need for an abundant measure of mercy. Since the measure with which we measure we will be measured back to us, Christ exhorts us to be merciful with

---

[4] Ibid.

others as our Father has been merciful with us. For mercy shared is mercy received. In this overflowing exchange of mercy, we not only bloom but indeed flourish like the Christ-vine's ecclesial branches lavishly filling the San Clemente apse.

Rome, 17 March 2014
The Second Monday of Lent
The Commemoration of Saint Patrick

XVIII

SAINT CLEMENT OF ROME, LENT 2015
Remaining in the Truth of Christ

Reading: Daniel 9:4-10
Psalm 78 (79)
Gospel: Luke 6:36-38

When I taught at the Jesuit High School in Tampa, Florida, I would remind the boys on the first day of class that God is both just and merciful. I would assure them that I hoped to be for them a paradigm of divine justice. If it was mercy they sought, they should go to the school chapel. I would conclude my opening remarks by quoting those immortal words of Dante Alighieri engraved above the gates of Hell: *Lasciate ogne speranza, voi ch'intrate* (DANTE, *Inferno*, Canto III.9).[1] Please do not misunderstand me. The high school classroom is a jungle. If one does not immediately tame the wild beasts who inhabit it, they will soon be having you for lunch. The university classroom, of course, is a different sort of jungle—admittedly less savage and more akin

---

[1] "Abandon every hope, you who enter here."

to a sleepy hollow. But even there on the first day of lectures I have had to employ certain, more subtle tactics to encourage, let us say, my students' disciplined participation. Let us be frank: the Old Adam remains alive and well even in seminarians!

Just as I would remind my students, the prophet Daniel exclaims: "Justice, O Lord, is on your side; we are shamefaced even to this day. ... But yours, O Lord, our God, are compassion and forgiveness" (Daniel 4:7,9).[2] With contrite hearts we, poor sinners, stand humbly before the good Lord who loves us passionately. As Pope Benedict XVI reminds us in *Deus Caritas Est*, God's passionate love is a forgiving love "so great that it turns God against himself, his love against his justice" (BENEDICT XVI, *Deus Caritas Est* §10). We might find Benedict's words initially jarring, for they seem to imply that mercy ousts justice. We might even be tempted to interpret today's Gospel in a similar fashion. For in commanding us to be merciful as our heavenly Father is merciful and to forgive in order that we might be forgiven, Jesus insists that we neither judge nor condemn. But if mercy is diametrically opposed to justice, then, God, who is both just and merciful, would indeed be divided against Himself. But the Triune God is One, and indivisible in His simplicity. His justice is His mercy, and vice versa. On this account, we must seek a deeper unity underlying the astonishing contrast which Pope Benedict poetically notes.

---

[2] Scriptural translation from the *New American Bible*.

All acts of mercy and forgiveness—both human and divine—follow upon a judgment. Without that previous judgment, our merciful acts would be rendered meaningless. For, we only forgive what we have judged offensive. Of course, we cannot judge the state of another's soul nor whether his name be written in the Book of Life. Such judgment pertains to God alone. In this regard, Jesus commands us to stop judging and condemning. But, in commanding us to be merciful as our heavenly Father is merciful, Jesus calls us by His grace to share in the Father's righteousness, that is, in His *iustitia*. We fulfill Jesus' command when we engage in those spiritual works of mercy which include admonishing sinners, bearing wrongs patiently and forgiving offenses willingly. Clearly, such spiritual works do not pit mercy against justice. On the contrary, when performing these spiritual works of mercy, we quite legitimately and indeed necessarily judge as wrongful the act to be born patiently and the offense to be forgiven willingly.

When we lose sight of the complementary nature of justice and mercy, we risk erroneously equating mercy with that false, utterly relativistic notion of tolerance rampant today in Western society whose prime directive is quite simply to live and let live. But such fallacious tolerance has nothing to do with Christian mercy. The ancient Church, for example, tolerated serious sinners in her midst in order to correct them and to call them to conversion, not to affirm them in their sin and to ease their path to perdition. Saint Augustine of Hippo's pastoral counsel to his fifth-century flock is no less pertinent today. "Bear with sinners," the

Bishop of Hippo exhorts,

> not by loving their sin, but by attacking their sin for their sake. Love sinners, not as sinners but as people. Just as if you love a sick person you attack the fever; if you spare the fever, you don't love the sick person. So tell your brother what the truth is, don't keep silent. What else am I doing but telling you what the truth is? Don't do it with little lies; tell him what the truth is openly and frankly—but until he correct himself, he must be borne with (AUGUSTINE OF HIPPO, *Sermon* 4.20).[3]

A dynamic exchange between justice and mercy characterizes Christian tolerance in imitation of our heavenly Father whose justice fuels His mercy. In this regard, Pope Benedict's 'turning against' is properly understood as an 'orienting towards'. God's justice is the driving force behind his passionately forgiving love. In His just mercy and merciful justice, God neither ignores those sins which separate us from Himself, nor does He desire to leave us wallowing in the misery which they have justly merited. Rather "God so loved the world that he gave his only Son, that whoever believes in him should not perish but have eternal life" (John 3:16). As the Scriptures reveal, the Father's mercy is the truth

---

[3] AUGUSTINE OF HIPPO, *Sermons*, vol. 1, *The Works of Saint Augustine: A translation for the 21st Century*, trans. EDMUND HILL, O.P., ed. JOHN E. ROTELLE, O.S.A. (Brooklyn: New City Press, 1990), p. 196.

of Christ which sets us free. Similarly, as we strive with the help of Christ's grace to imitate our merciful Father, justice rightly fuels our mercy when we forgive those who have trespassed against us. We love our neighbor, who has fallen into sin, not by withholding the truth from him, but rather by proclaiming the truth of Christ which justly calls us all to continual conversion as it mercifully sets us free. Only by remaining in the truth of Christ, then, do we learn to be merciful as our Father is merciful.

Rome, 2 March 2015
The Second Monday of Lent

XIX

CHRIST TEMPTED IN THE DESERT
Humbly persevering in the priesthood

Gospel: Matthew 4:1-11

If during His life Jesus not only did not sin, but indeed could not have sinned, then to what extent, if at all, did He suffer temptation? Did not His inability to sin effectively render any possible temptation meaningless? How can we speak of His being tempted in the desert if there was no fear of His ever sinning? Is the evangelical scene simply an elaborate fiction concocted to give us the false impression that like us Jesus struggled with temptation? When some students of theology first come across the doctrine of Christ's impeccability, they reject it immediately because it apparently denies Christ's true humanity and undermines His salvific mission. For, as the more astute student among them will note in reference to our fallen humanity's proclivity towards sin, "that which he has not assumed he has not healed" (GREGORY OF NAZIANZUS, *Letter* 101.32).[1] In their laudable yet, in this regard, misguided at-

---

[1] GREGORY OF NAZIANZUS "Letters on the Apollinarian Controversy," *Christology of the Later Fathers*, trans. CHARLES GORDON BROWNE and

tempts to defend Christ's true humanity, they appeal to the *Letter to the Hebrews* which attests that "we have not a high priest who is unable to sympathize with our weaknesses, but one who in every respect has been tempted as we are, yet without sin" (Hebrews 4:15). They are quick to agree, of course, that Jesus did not sin. But, for Jesus to be truly human, He Himself had to have been able to sin. He had to have suffered like us from the throes of concupiscence. Like Saint Paul—and indeed, like every man and woman who have lived ever since that tragic day when Eve gave Adam that apple to eat—Jesus had to have experienced the interior battle of a disordered will divided against itself (cf. Romans 7:15-24). He had to have struggled to do the good even though unlike us He Himself never failed to accomplish it. In sum, in order for Jesus' temptations to have been real, He like us had to have been capable of sinning.

The fallacy of this argument lies in its equation of the ability to sin with being fully human. God did not create man a sinner. Indeed, at his creation, man enjoyed the grace of being able not to sin (*posse non peccare*), and he was called to everlasting communion with his Creator. Our fallen state is not the true measure of our humanity. Sin does not make us human. Rather, it dehumanizes us. Jesus' impeccability does not detract from His humanity. On the contrary, it assures it in its fullness. "In reality it is only in the mystery of the Word made flesh that the mystery of man truly becomes clear. For Adam, the first man, was a type of him who was to come,

---

JAMES EDWARD SWALLOW, ed. EDWARD R. HARDY (Philadelphia: The Westminster Press, 1954), p. 218.

Christ the Lord. Christ the new Adam, in the very revelation of the mystery of the Father and of his love, fully reveals man to himself and brings to light his most high calling" (Vatican II, *Gaudium et Spes* § 22).

In His humanity Jesus enjoyed the grace of impeccability (*non posse peccare*). He enjoyed it in virtue of the hypostatic union. Jesus Christ is the Divine Word Incarnate—one Person (the Second Person of the Most Holy Trinity) in two natures, human and divine. Each nature has its own will. Therefore, Jesus has both a divine will, which is the one divine will of the Father, Son and Holy Spirit, and a human will, which operates in perfect harmony with His divine will. In His one Person, Christ's two natures are present without confusion, without change, without division and without separation (cf. *The Chalcedonian Definition of the Faith*, Denzinger § 302). To say that Jesus could have sinned, that His human will could have rejected and turned against His divine will, would be to introduce the possibility of division into His one Person. But such a possibility, even if only a theoretical possibility, cannot be admitted without denying the indivisibility of the hypostatic union. Hence, not only do we profess in faith that Jesus never sinned, but indeed that He was incapable of sinning.

Nonetheless, the question, with which we began, remains: if there was no fear of Jesus ever sinning, then, how could He have been truly tempted? As our more astute student, rightly appealing to *Hebrews*, will remind us, that Jesus endured temptation, that He shared our experience of being tempted, is an essential part of His redemptive mission. In our response, we must maintain both Jesus' impeccability

157

and the veracity of His temptations. An attentive reading of the evangelical text will reveal that, while being truly tempted in the desert, Jesus was not being tempted to sin. For, the Evil One's proposals were not in and of themselves sinful—at least not for Jesus.

The devil prefaces his first two challenges to Jesus, saying: "If you are the Son of God..." "If you are the Son of God," he insists, "then, change stones into bread or else cause the angels to come to your aid." In other words, Satan demands that Jesus manifest His divine power. In the third temptation, the devil shows Him "all the kingdoms of the world and the glory of them" (Matthew 4:8), promising to give them to Him if He should fall down in worship before him. Although such idolatrous worship is thoroughly detestable, it does not constitute the final temptation. Rather, the glory of earth's kingdoms does. While all three are real temptations, none of them entails sin, for Jesus truly is the Son of God, the King of kings and Lord of lords (cf. Revelation 19:16). He does not sin when He exercises the divine power which is His. When He miraculously multiplied those five loaves and two fish at Tabgha in order to feed the five thousand in the wilderness (cf. Matthew 14:13-21; Mark 6:30-44), He did not sin. Had He turned stones into bread in the wilderness beyond the Jordan, He would not have sinned. Had Jesus caused the angels to bear Him up upon their hands "lest [He] strike [His] foot against a stone" (Matthew 4:6), He would not have sinned. For, if He had so desired, Jesus the Creator and Lord of the heavenly hosts could have called upon the angels to come to His defense. As Jesus would later rhetorically remind a sword-wielding

Simon Peter in the Garden of Gethsemane: "Do you think that I cannot appeal to my Father, and he will at once send me more than twelve legions of angels?" (Matthew 26:53). Finally, Christ the King, whose kingship transcends all worldly kingdoms (cf. John 18:36), reigns from the beginning over all the earth and indeed the entire creation. Earth's kingdoms possess no true glory which is not already rightfully His own. Had He chosen to lay manifest claim to His regal glory, He would not have sinned. In sum, at each instance, Jesus was clearly not being tempted to sin—something that he could not have done—, but He was, nonetheless, truly tempted. So, wherein lies the temptation?

The devil challenged Jesus to change the modality of His mission. He tempted Him to abandon His self-abasement, His *kenosis*—that is, to forsake the humble path, which He had chosen, and to reveal His divine power immediately. But "Christ Jesus, who, though he was in the form of God, did not count equality with God a thing to be grasped, but emptied himself, taking the form of a servant, being born in the likeness of men. And found in human form he humbled himself and became obedient unto death, even death on a cross" (Philippians 2:6-8). Obedient though He was, He did not approach His death without fear. His agony in the Garden of Gethsemane poignantly reveals that as a man Jesus did experience the natural, although not sinful, fears which His self-abasement entailed. Human beings naturally fear death. As Saint Maximus the Confessor explains, the suffering, which arises from the natural fear of death, is neither sinful in itself nor does it lead one away from God (cf. MAXIMUS THE CONFESSOR, *Opuscula Theologica et Polemica* 32-33 (PG 91,

66-70)). "Sorrowful, even to death" (Mark 14:34), Jesus did not sin when He prayed: "Abba, Father, all things are possible to thee; remove this cup from me" (Mark 14:36a). Nor did His fear lead Him away from the Father to whom He prayed immediately afterwards: "Yet not what I will, but what thou wilt" (Mark 14:36b). As Christ experienced the natural fear of death with its concomitant temptation to change the modality of His mission, His human will remained ever steadfast in its harmonious cooperation with the divine will which is His with the Father and the Holy Spirit. Although truly tempted Jesus remained ever faithful to the modality of His mission. For, otherwise, "how then should the scriptures be fulfilled, that it must be so?" (Matthew 26:54).

Satan's attempts to tempt Christ in the desert parallel his earlier, lamentably successful seductions in the Garden of Eden. In that garden the serpent tragically persuaded Adam and Eve to change the modality of their divine call, which resulted in mankind's Fall. God had created man for communion with Himself. He desired to share with humanity His own divinity through His Son's Incarnation. As Joseph Ratzinger once preached, "God created the universe in order to be able to become a human being and pour out his love upon us and to invite us to love him in return."[2] Indeed, God became man so that man, in turn, might become God (cf. IRENAEUS OF LYONS, *Adversus Haereses* 3.16.3;

---

[2] JOSEPH RATZINGER, *In the Beginning…: A Catholic Understanding of the Story of Creation and the Fall*, Second Homily, trans. BONIFACE RAMSEY, O.P. (Edinburgh: T & T Clark, 1995), p. 30.

ATHANASIUS, *De Incarnatione* 54.3; THOMAS AQUINAS, *Opuscula* 57, 1-4). In the Son, who is divine by nature, man becomes divine by adoption. But our first parents proved impatient. They did not wish to wait for this gift to be given. Rather, they wanted to take it directly for themselves. They wanted to be like God, to gain knowledge of good and evil—but on their own terms. This, however, is impossible. For, man cannot possibly make himself God. He has no natural right to lay claim to God's gracious gift of divinization—a pure gift freely given and owed to no one. Nonetheless, deceived by the devil, our first parents rejected their creatureliness. They sought to set aside the humility of our human condition in order to grasp after divine glory. Seduced by Satan, they attempted to change the modality by which they were to receive the gift of divinization, and by this means they lost it.

Adam and Eve's attempt to change the modality of their divinization was devastatingly sinful for the entire human race. In order to redeem us, the Father sent us His only-begotten Son. The Divine Word made man was born in the likeness of our sinful flesh (cf. Romans 8:3). Through His Incarnation He entered into our world, and though sinless, took upon Himself our sinfulness. In the desert He endured the very temptation which had derailed the human race. But had Jesus changed the modality of His mission, He would not have sinned. For, He, who is the Son of God, does not sin in being Himself and revealing His divinity before men. He could have chosen to save us by a means other than the Cross. But He came among us to remedy our pride by His humility. In order that the Scriptures should be fulfilled (cf. Matthew 26:54), He resisted all temptations to the contrary, vehemently rebuking even Peter for having suggested otherwise: "Get behind me, Satan! You are a hindrance to me: for you are not on the side of God, but of men" (Matthew 16:23). The temptation to change the modality of one's vocation is unfortunately not foreign to priests who, though serving *in persona Christi capitis*, are no less than their fellow man the sons of Adam and Eve.

Like Christ we priests can also be tempted to set aside the humility of our sacerdotal service. But in our case it is pride and vainglory which blind us to the Crucified Lord, whom we serve, and lead us like Adam and Eve to lay claim to a glory not our own. Unlike Christ we do suffer from the throes of concupiscence. We experience within ourselves the divided will of which Saint Paul wrote. The grace of Christ's impeccability (*non posse peccare*), which awaits us in heaven, is not yet ours here on earth. Seeking ourselves and our own pleasure, we sin. Our sins undermine and threaten to destroy our sacerdotal mission. Scandal impedes our evangelical service. How easily we can be discouraged and tempted to abandon our mission! But let us never forget that Christ Jesus Himself was also tempted—truly tempted even though without sin—to abandon the humility of His own mission. On this account, He sympathizes deeply with us in our temptations either to change the modality of our mission or even to abandon it all together. For our part, "since…we have a great high priest who has passed through the heavens, Jesus the Son of God, let us hold fast our confession" (Hebrews 4:14)—let us remain steadfast in our humble sacerdotal service. "For we have not a high priest who is unable to sympathize with our weaknesses, but one who in every respect has been tempted as we are, yet without sin. Let us then with confidence draw near to the throne of grace, that we may receive mercy and find grace to help in time of need" (Hebrews 4:15-16). Here Saint Augustine's wise counsel is particularly pertinent to the priest under diabolical attack: "In [Jesus] recognize yourself being put to the proof by temptation, and then recognize yourself winning the fight in him" (AUGUSTINE OF HIPPO, *Expositions of the Psalms* 60.3).[3]

In Eden man's primordial temptation was to change the modality of his vocation. In the desert Jesus suffered the same temptation. In the wilderness of today's world, priests are not immune from it. Adam and Eve succumbed to it. Christ triumphed over it, and, by His redeeming grace, we priests can resist it, persevering in our humble ministry not for our own glory, but for the glory of God and the salvation of the world.[4]

Villa Palazzola, 9 March 2014
The First Sunday of Lent

---

[3] AUGUSTINE OF HIPPO, *Expositions of the Psalms*, vol. 3, trans. MARIA BOULDING, O.S.B. (Hyde Park: New City Press, 2001), p. 194.
[4] "Pour la gloire de Dieu et le salut du monde"—the response of the faithful in French to the *Orate, fratres* of Holy Mass.

XX

LENTEN VESPERS

Running so as to win the incorruptible crown of eternal life

Reading: 1 Corinthians 9:24-25

In the short reading, which comes from Saint Paul's *First Letter to the Corinthians*, the Apostle offers us an athletic analogy in order that we might understand better our Christian pilgrimage towards our heavenly homeland. Every athlete, who participates in the stadium races, runs so as to win the prize which goes to one alone. On this account, he is temperate in all things. He rejects all that is not physically healthy. He dominates his own body in order that his body respond with great docility to his every command. Only such psycho-physical excellence wins the prize. If an athlete disciplines himself in this manner in order to win a merely corruptible crown, how much more ought we Christians train ourselves in order to win an incorruptible crown, that is, to gain eternal life?

Saint Paul disciplines himself in order to engage without reserve in this salvific race. As he explains to the Corinthians: "Well, I do not run aimlessly, I do not box as one beating the air; but I pommel my body and subdue it, lest after preaching to others I myself should be disqualified" (1 Corinthians 9:26-27). "I appeal to you therefore, brethren, by the mercies of God," he writes to the Romans, "to present your bodies as a living sacrifice, holy and acceptable to God, which is your spiritual worship. Do not be conformed to this world but be transformed by the renewal of your mind, that you may prove what is the will of God, what is good and acceptable and perfect" (Romans 12:1-2). By his own example, Saint Paul calls us to discipline our bodies for the salvific good of our souls in order that we may know and accomplish God's will. He exhorts us to order our carnal desires according to right reason and not according to the world's perverse mentality in order that we may win the prize of eternal life.

That is all well and good. But how often do we ourselves lament that such spiritually athletic prowess escapes us! How poorly do we succeed in offering our bodies as a living sacrifice truly pleasing to God! How many times do our attempts to castigate our bodies for the good of our souls fail! It is not by chance that only one wins that corruptible crown in the stadium. Such self-sacrificing devotion on the part of the athlete is not ordinary. Common men do not possess it, or at least rarely do they persevere in their attempts to achieve it. "No pain, no gain" may inspire some, but it fails to motivate many. Given that the prize awaiting the Christian is far greater than that corruptible crown awarded to the victorious athlete, how much greater is the force necessary to win it and how much shorter do we fall in our efforts! What hope, therefore, remains for us poor sinners? We should honestly say that as regards our salvation the athletic analogy would fail if everything depended totally upon our naked strength. Thankfully, Saint Paul was not a Pelagian.

The Apostle instructs the Philippians: "God is at work in you, both to will and to work for his good pleasure" (Philippians 2:13). The desire to run the Christian race and the strength exerted in the actual running come from God. It is He who calls us to run and He who gives us the grace to embrace all the sacrifices of our Christian pilgrimage. Without Him and His grace, we could not control our carnal desires in order to win that incorruptible crown which is eternal life. At the end of this Christian race when God will reward our efforts, our merits, He will do nothing other than crown His own gifts (cf. AUGUSTINE OF HIPPO, *Letter* 186.10). On this account, Saint Paul asks each of the Corinthians: "What have you that you did not receive? If then you received it, why do you boast as if it were not a gift" (1 Corinthians 4:7)?

In this same light Saint Augustine confesses: "There can be no hope for me except in your great mercy. Give me the grace to do as you command, and command me to do what you will" (AUGUSTINE OF HIPPO, *Confessions* 10.29)![1] *Da quod iubes et iube quod vis.* Pelagius detested this particular saying of Augustine above all else. For, Pelagius was a rigorous spiritual athlete. He strove by means of his own unaided

---

[1] AUGUSTINE OF HIPPO, *Confessions*, trans. R. S. PINE-COFFIN (New York: Penguin Books, 1961), p. 233.

strength to win that prize which man without God's help can, in fact, never obtain. Yes, it is true that a penitential spirit ought to define our Christian pilgrimage. Christians are rightly temperate and even ascetical. In fact, God commands continence, that is, self-mastery, of us all. But, as Saint Augustine, quoting the *Book of Wisdom*, observes: "No man can be master of himself, except of God's bounty" (Ibid.; cf. Wisdom 8:21). Without God's help our struggles to control our carnal desires and order them according to right reason prove futile. The hope to succeed in this spiritual enterprise is not to be found in ourselves, but rather in the Lord and His mercy. Our hope is in the One who gives both the desire and the doing.

The God-given gift of continence properly orders our souls to their unique and highest Good. It liberates us from the multiplicity of carnal desires and orients our otherwise restless hearts towards their only true peace. Thus does Christ's grace purify our hearts so that we may see God and adore Him alone. This vision of God is the unique goal of the Christian athlete who with Christ's grace wins the prize of eternal life. Concluding his confession Augustine exclaims: "O Charity, my God, set me on fire with your love! You command me to be continent. Give me the grace to do as you command, and command me to do what you will" (*Confessions* 10.29)! We are able to make a similar self-offering free from all anxiety because we know in faith that all does not depend upon ourselves, but rather upon the Lord's grace with which we cooperate. We hope not in ourselves, but rather in the Cross of Our Lord Jesus Christ. *O Crux, ave, spes unica!* The Holy Cross is indeed our only hope, for upon

It is nailed the Crucified Christ who mercifully bathes us in His Blood which restores our life by the forgiveness of our sins. His loving sacrifice upon the Cross makes every life-giving sacrifice of ours possible. Our grace-inspired sacrifices, in turn, strengthen us so that like Saint Paul we may run the race in order to win the incorruptible crown of everlasting life!

Rome, 11 March 2012
The Third Sunday of Lent

XXI

SAINT THOMAS THE APOSTLE
Joyfully professing the paschal faith within the Church

Gospel: John 20:19-29

On that first Easter night, the Risen Lord Jesus Cruci-fied appeared among His disciples who had anxiously locked themselves behind closed doors. His greeting of peace dis-pelled their fear. His wounded hands and side spoke elo-quently to them of that love than which there is no greater, of that perfect love which casts out all fear. The Resurrection had transformed these ignoble signs into signs of victory— the victory of love over death, the victory of his mercy over our sins. Breathing His Holy Spirit upon them, He shared the power of this victory with His disciples, entrusting to them His own mission of reconciliation. As the Father had sent Him, He sent them into the world to exercise the power of the keys not only to bind but most especially to loose sin-ners—to extend the power of his Resurrection to the ends of the earth.

The Apostle Thomas was absent from their company that night. Upon his return, the other disciples shared their joy with him, proclaiming to their brother our paschal faith in the Lord's Resurrection: "We have seen the Lord" (John 20:25). But Thomas stubbornly refused to believe. Until he himself beheld the signs of Christ's victory, he would not believe. His individual 'I' of disbelief stood opposed to the communal 'We' of faith. Throughout that first Easter Octave, the other disciples rejoiced while Thomas remained faithless. How deep his misery must have been! For the Easter faith is an ecclesial faith. The disciples collectively encountered the Risen Lord in the Upper Room where they had previously shared the first Eucharist with Him. The mission of reconciliation, which Jesus imparted to His disciples, is an ecclesial mission to bind and loose, reconciling the sinner to God within the Church. The Spirit, whom Jesus breathed forth upon His disciples, is the Divine Spirit who unites the community of disciples together in love. The entire evangelical scene witnesses to both the ecclesial nature of the faith and the mission given that night to the Apostles. Thomas failed to profess this Easter faith and to share in his brothers' joy because he stood apart from their brotherhood. Removed from ecclesial communion, as it were, Thomas lacked the faith and joy which was theirs. But on the Octave of Easter, Jesus appeared again to His disciples in the Upper Room. On this occasion Thomas was with them. Again the Risen Christ bestowed His peace upon them and revealed to Thomas the victorious signs of His mercy. Standing in the midst of this apostolic ecclesial community, Jesus exhorted Thomas: "Do not be faithless, but believing" (John 20:27). United with his brothers Thomas immediately professed the Church's faith in Christ Jesus: "My Lord and my God" (John 20:28)!

As Saint John's Gospel reveals, Christian faith has never been nor can it ever be simply a matter of "Me and Jesus". Our Christian faith in the Paschal Mystery is from the very beginning communally professed. "*We* have seen the Lord," the disciples announced to Thomas. Thomas himself only came to profess the Easter faith when he encountered the Risen Lord in the company of his brothers gathered together in the Cenacle, the place of ecclesial communion *par excellence*. For, it was there that Christ had offered the first Eucharist, the source and summit of the Church's life. Within those same walls, the Spirit would give birth to the Universal Church on Pentecost Sunday.

In his life and ministry the priest is called to profess and witness to the Easter faith within the Church. He is called by the Lord through the Church to Holy Orders for the sake of an ecclesial ministry. His faithful witness and ministry builds up the faith of the Church. But in terms of his own personal experience of faith, the priest does not simply minister to others. He receives as well. His own faith is also nourished within the community which he serves. It is likewise nurtured by the fraternity which he shares with his brother priests. A priest, who removes himself from the support of priestly fraternity and the broader ecclesial community, places his faith and his ministry at risk. Having been away from the apostolic brotherhood on that first Easter night, Thomas failed to profess the Church's paschal faith. Indeed, even when his brothers attempted to share their faith with him, he obstinately rejected it. He refused the gift of faith. Thus he remained not only faithless, but also joyless. Only once he had encountered the Risen Lord within that apostolic band of brothers was he able to rejoice with them and profess the Church's faith in the Risen Christ.

This *Year of Faith* calls priests, along with all the baptized faithful, to nurture the gift of faith which they have received from the Lord. From the very beginning the gift of Christian faith has been received within a community of believers. It thrives within ecclesial communion outside of which it withers and fades. This year of grace provides priests not only with an opportunity to share their faith with their communities, but also to allow their own faith to be strengthened by the holy faithful whom they serve. Most especially this year calls priests to follow the example of the Apostles gathered together in the Upper Room on that first Easter night. May priests rejoice together in their common profession of faith in the Risen Lord Jesus Crucified, and may they sustain one another in that faith, especially in times of trial. In this way Christ's joy will be theirs, and their joy will be complete.

Vatican City, Easter 2013

Finito di stampare nel mese di Maggio 2015
presso Mediagraf Spa - Noventa Padovana (PD)